HOW TO
TRIUMPH
OVER
TRIVIA

HOW TO TRIUMPH OVER TRIVIA

Learning to Follow Life's
Significant Pursuits

LINDA SCHOTT

Christian Communications
P.O. Box 150
Nashville, TN 37202

Published by Christian Communications
A division of the Gospel Advocate Co.
P.O. Box 150, Nashville, TN 37202

ISBN 0-89225-364-9

Contents

Lesson One

The World As I See It

You might call me an eternal optimist. I refuse to worry about the national debt, and I'm certain we're headed for world peace. The drought will be over soon; cures for AIDS and cancer will soon be discovered; and by the time I'm 70, heart disease will not even exist.

In most circumstances I expect the good. That's why, in the past, I tended to ignore doomsday prophecies of the coming century. However, recent world events have caused me to question the reality of my Pollyanna attitude—an attitude shared by many in today's Christian community. We want desperately to believe the words of Robert Browning: "God's in His heaven . . . all's right with the world."

Is all right with the world? We are slaughtering 1.5 million unborn babies a year. Children can't pray in school. The incidence of drug abuse has skyrocketed. God's name is blasphemed on television daily in millions of homes. We're destroying our national resources and depleting water and food supplies rapidly. Even the ocean is no longer safe for marine life because it has become the world's dumping ground.

Have our immature and unrealistic attitudes toward world problems contributed to the deplorable state of today's society?

During World War II, Christians in Nazi Germany ignored the slaughter of six million Jews. The Christians thought their place was in the churches, singing and praying. Are we falling into the same pattern? While we've been busy attempting to maintain family and home, build material success, and love God and country, the moral foundations of this great land have been crumbling under our feet.

We've been hoping others would take care of this godless and immoral world—the world that is to be the inheritance of our children. We've chosen to close our eyes to many critical issues.

The Good-Life Syndrome

Nothing seems to matter in our society but the accumulation of wealth. We're crushed under loads of what we consider the "essentials" of life. We purchase *things* to remind ourselves of how successful we are—cars, homes, jewelry, stocks, bonds, etc. Somewhere along this futile journey we lose our children in the shuffle of materialism. Where have all the children gone? The time to ask that question and to find some answers is now.

Emphasis on Youthfulness and Beauty

Anorexia . . . bulimia . . . steroids . . . anti-aging creams. . . a tuck here, a lift there. All these are either health problems resulting from the obsessive desire to be thin or remedies designed to lead us to the eternal fountain of youth.

Plastic surgery has become a status symbol. Clothes have become tools to get what we want in life. We wrap ourselves in beautiful packages and forget that it's what's on the inside that counts.

Morality

We use watered-down terms to erase the concept of evil. Robert Welch, in an article in *Focus on the Family* magazine gives examples of these "euphemistic smoke screens":

"living in sin" = "meaningful relationships"
"chastity" = "neurotic inhibition"
"self-indulgence" = "self-fulfillment"
"abortion" = "choice"
"adultery" = "non-monogamy"[1]

Pornography and child sexual abuse are common topics of news reports and programs. X-rated movies are available to every age on cable television. Sex is used to sell everything from hot tubs to children's clothes. AIDS threatens to destroy our nation. Promiscuity and homosexuality parade in the streets of America.

We watch the parade go by, and our hearts are saddened. Yet we are falsely secure that "someone else" can turn things around.

Television

We spend more than 1,200 hours a year viewing television. Two sexual acts occur on each daily soap opera, and most are adulterous. Countless acts of violence are committed during a few hours of viewing.

On any given night my family can flip through the television channels and view intimate bedroom scenes, hear off-color humor about sex and homosexuality, watch a rape in progress, see nudity, and hear newlyweds discuss their latest lovemaking techniques.

Our intellects are insulted as advertisements lead us to believe that wearing designer jeans will bring the men running—or that we need to color our hair because "we're worth it."

Rock Music

Our children are mesmerized by the music they hear. They sit for endless hours hooked up to headphones, hypnotized by lyrics that glamorize rape, murder, violence, suicide, drugs and alcohol.

Education

A war is going on in the classrooms of America. Students murder fellow students in senseless fits of rage, or they take out their frustrations on underpaid classroom teachers.

Gary Bauer, in *Focus on the Family* magazine, cited a 10-year-old study on violence in the schools. The National Institute of Education found in 1978 that each month in secondary schools, 282,000 students were attacked; 2.4 million students had personal property stolen; 1,000 teachers were assaulted and needed medical attention; and 125,000 students and teachers were threatened with physical harm.[2]

Schools are overcrowded, and some don't even have enough textbooks for every child. Piles of curricula, required by the state, leave no time for the teacher to pursue creativity with the children. Teachers do more policing than teaching. Textbooks are stripped of values, morals and Christian ethics, and the absence of these morals help undermine family values.

The Demise of the American Family

Only 7 percent of American families are structured in the traditional model of employed father and homemaking mother. Approximately 42 million women work outside the home. Many with young children are forced to resort to incompetent child care. Often older children are left at home unsupervised for long periods of time.

Isolationism

Who is our neighbor? Who is our friend? We're tired, so we pull in and become couch potatoes. Most of us don't know or care what's happening in the home next door or down the street. Friendship is a time-consuming luxury most of us can't afford.

Lesson One

Questions

1. What do you think is the most important issue of our time?
2. Why do we, as Christians, tend to be uninvolved with social and political issues?
3. What role can women play in bringing about necessary changes in this country?
4. Share with the class any political or social activities in which you have been involved.
5. Plan now, as a class, specific activities to make your voice heard in the land.

Notes Lesson One

[1]Robert Welch, *Focus on the Family* (January 1988).
[2]Gary Bauer, *Focus on the Family* (July 1988).

Lesson Two

In Pursuit of Riches

As a child I spent many hours browsing through the poetry, essays and beautiful pictures in *Ideals* magazine. The scenery was breathtaking, but even more impressive were the pictures of the family. Mom, Dad and the kids were always shown gathered around the Christmas tree, seated at a table laden with a turkey and all the trimmings, or stretched out on a lovely blanket enjoying a picnic in the woods. Surrounding the family was an almost invisible "rosy" glow that suggested peace, warmth and security.

The family in the picture was the perfect American all-is-well, life-is-beautiful, apple-pie, homespun family.

Ideals magazine is still around, and the pictures are just as beautiful, but much has happened since the '60s to tarnish the image of the American family. The tarnishing began with the television.

In the '50s, Robert Young, in "Father Knows Best," portrayed a father with wisdom, love and good humor. A couple of decades later he had been replaced by J.R. Ewing on *Dallas*—the greedy oil baron who let nothing come between himself and his fortune. He was to become the role model for millions of American men. Television helped give birth to our quest for the life-style of the rich and famous!

Other television series had begun to pick up the theme, and riches became the barometer of success. The American public bought it. We soon began to dream of earthly mansions, big cars and designer clothing. Our dream became one of buying, getting and owning to obtain happiness.

As I write this, I look around at my surroundings. A baby grand piano stands in the middle of my moderately decorated living room. My furniture is comfortable and clean. Just last week I purchased a chaise chair for my over-sized bedroom and a beautiful print for my wall.

I love my home; it speaks of warmth and care and love of beauty. This home is the refuge of four people who return to it daily to be nourished and loved and re-energized.

Yet, if one of the homeless of our nation were to step through my door, could I justify to him my comfortable home? Am I enjoying this home and my possessions entirely too much? How much is too much?

Jesus' View of Wealth

Jesus, our model in all realms of life, chose a lifestyle free of riches. All He owned were the clothes He wore on His back.

Paul, in 2 Corinthians 8:9, reminds us of the Christ's attitude toward wealth: "For you know the grace of our Lord Jesus Christ, that though he was rich, yet for your sakes he became poor, so that you through his poverty might become rich."

Jesus urged His followers to look for happiness outside the realm of earthly possessions:

> Do not store up for yourselves treasures on earth, where moth and rust destroy, and where thieves break in and steal. But store up for yourselves treasures in heaven, where moth and rust do not destroy, and where thieves do not break in and steal. For where your treasure is, there your heart will be also (Matthew 6:19-21).

To walk with God when your heart is walking with riches—when what you own or hope to own is your major concern—is not easy. Everything you do centers on the accumulation of more wealth.

In Ecclesiastes 5:10 we learn that "Whoever loves money never has money enough; whoever loves wealth is never satisfied with his income. This too is meaningless."

The More You Accumulate, The More You Need!

Contentment Without Riches

As Christians, we should be content with simply having food, clothing, and shelter to sustain us from day to day. Our problems begin when we see these provisions as inadequate and want to move up the rungs on the ladder of success and materialism. Satan wants us to think there is always more waiting—a better job, a bigger house, a sleek new car, and so on.

He also does a pretty good job of tossing in jealousy and envy as part of the package of discontent. Is it difficult for you to look at the lifestyle of the rich and famous without feeling a twinge of lust for what they possess?

The following verses from 1 Timothy 6:6-8 speak to us about contentment without wealth:

> But godliness with contentment is great
> gain. For we brought nothing into the

world, and we can take nothing out of it.
But if we have food and clothing, we will
be content with that. People who want
to get rich fall into temptation and a trap
and into many foolish and harmful desires
that plunge men into ruin and destruction.
For the love of money is a root of all kinds
of evil. Some people, eager for money,
have wandered from the faith and pierced
themselves with many griefs.

You can probably relate to the story of Angie
(not her real name but a true story). Angie
landed a successful marketing job that required
travel away from her family and association
with many people high on the social ladder.
Within six months she had left her husband and
three small children, found another man, and
was a swinging member of the jet set. Angie
gave in to the temptations of greed and immorality. Her husband was a deacon in the church.
His life and the lives of three precious children
were destroyed, all for the sake of wealth, power
and status.

On the opposite extreme is Beth, who left a
job and a promotion in order to devote all of
her time and energy to the care of her family.
As a result, her family had to move down a
notch in material expectations. They have begun
wearing less fancy clothes, have curtailed expen-
sive social events, and have traded the family

Olds for a Chevette. The result of the change is one growing, happy family, united in a common purpose.

Are you an Angie or a Beth?

If you work outside the home, are you doing so to increase possessions or to provide food, clothing and shelter for your family?

The issue of "working" moms is a highly volatile one. The mention of it can trigger explosive arguments. The working mother issue can be decided only by husband and wife. The choice is a highly personal one, and none outside the home have the right to make judgments on those who must make that decision.

An interesting fact to note, however, is that more and more "superwomen" are feeling worn down and generally discontented. They are rapidly being replaced by what is called the "sequencer"—the mom who establishes herself in a career, interrupts it to have children and stay at home with them through the preschool years, and resumes work when they are school age. (*The Sunday Tennessean*, October 9, 1988, "The Sequencer," by Vickie Kilgore.)

I was a sequencer. I returned to the teaching profession when my children began elementary school. Although I would recommend being a sequencer to young mothers, yet even that was not a perfect situation. I had the best of two worlds; I had a job where I could be with my children, taking them to school, bringing them home, keeping the same hours, and having the same vacations. Yet, those years were some of the most difficult and exhausting of my life, and I often wonder if I would do it again.

If I had chosen not to be a sequencer, would I have been as content with furniture and clothing from the local discount stores? Or would I have been one of those women who nags her husband constantly for more and more material possessions? You've seen this type of woman. She whines about the furniture, a house that's too small, the lack of designer clothing hanging in the closet, or the fact that the family can't take a six-week cruise to the Caribbean. Of course, some men have similar materialistic desires. Many of them demand that the wife work so that they can have the luxuries they desire, which might include a power boat, a four-wheel-drive Jeep, or maybe a Rolex watch.

Remember, "godliness with contentment is great gain. . . ." That verse is a personal call to each of us to be content with present financial circumstances. The message is pretty tough for those of us who love pretty clothes and comfortable surroundings!

Read and study Proverbs 31 in your own Bible for a picture of a truly wealthy woman.

Lesson Two

Questions

1. Does God condemn riches? Locate and discuss some specific biblical passages about riches.
2. Did Jesus have any wealthy friends? Name them, and tell about their relationship to Him.
3. When do riches become a sin?
4. How do we often rationalize our desire for wealth?
5. What did the Queen of Sheba find out about riches from the wise ruler Solomon?
6. How can a marriage and family life be affected by the desire for wealth?
7. Below, list your reasons for working outside the home. Then spend some time in prayer about the matter.
8. Before class, write a personal paraphrase of Proverbs 31. Be prepared to share it with the class.

Further wisdom from Solomon regarding riches for your own private study: Proverbs 3:9-10; 11:28; 15:16; 22:2; 23:4, 5; 28:20-22.

Lesson Three

The Godly Use of Riches

Before you decide that you *have* no riches, remember that in the eyes of the world, every person who studies this book is quite wealthy. God has abundantly blessed our nation.

The following suggestions are for those who desire to be good stewards of their riches, no matter how great or small. "So if you have not been trustworthy in handling worldly wealth, who will trust you with true riches? And if you have not been trustworthy with someone else's property, who will give you property of your own (Luke 16:11, 12)?

1. Don't be conceited. As a teen, I attended a high school with many youth of affluent families. Those with wealth often looked with disdain on those who were not so blessed with worldly goods.

Unfortunately, many adults follow the same behavior patterns. Browsing in a department store during the Christmas rush last year, I observed a well-dressed woman step out of a limousine and come into the store. She shopped in a nearby department. She screamed and raved at the salesclerks because they would not wait on her quickly enough. After she caused much commotion and asked for the manager, the rest of us were put aside while she was gallantly rescued and rushed through the check-out counter. With a toss of her head, she grabbed her purchase and flitted back to her limousine, climbed in, and left in a blaze of her own glory.

The scene was similar to others I had viewed before. The wealthy often have a tendency to expect others to bow to every demand. They tend to have little patience with delay and don't seem to mind pushing others around to get what they want. They often look down on individuals lower on the rungs of the social ladder. Yet Luke 16:15 says, "What is highly valued among men is detestable in God's sight."

2. Remember that God is the source of your wealth. "Look to the rock from which you were cut and to the quarry from which you were hewn" (Isaiah 51:1). In school we call it "back to the basics."

It matters little to our God whether you have a luxurious home in the suburbs or a simple wooden shack in the inner-city. As we will study later, our ultimate goal in life is to love God and to glorify Him. If you possess great riches and have the temptation to look down on those who do not, try to remember that God has created everyone equal. The Christian attempting to walk with God is humbled by his or her material wealth and realizes that God is the "giver of all good and perfect gifts" (James 1:17).

3. Don't put your trust in riches. A false sense of security can shadow your reasoning and judgment. Solomon warns us about this in Proverbs 23:5: "Cast but a glance at riches, and they are gone, for they will surely sprout wings and fly off to the sky like an eagle."

In Ecclesiastes 5:13-15 he says:

> "I have seen a grievous evil under the sun: wealth hoarded to the harm of its owner, or wealth lost through some misfortune, so that when he has a son, there is nothing left for him. Naked a man comes from his mother's womb, and as he comes, so he departs. He takes nothing from his labor that he can carry in his hand."

These words are sad, indeed, for those who expend every living moment striving for the accumulation of wealth.

We've all read or heard stories about persons who face bankruptcy. I once knew a man who owned his own business. He worked day and night to build his empire. He pursued the "good" life with obsessive determination.

All was going well until the birth of the computer. Then his services were no longer marketable. Business fell off at a rapid rate. Within a year he had lost all of his earthly possessions. His wife was so embarrassed that she took their only child and moved to another city.

4. Return a portion of your riches to God. I was raised in a single-parent home. Times were rough, but some godly people in my congregation sent me each summer to a Christian camp in Searcy, AR. At that camp my values and morals were formed. Through loving examples and instruction, I grew into a very personal relationship with Jesus Christ. To those who put in a dollar or two to send me, it was but a little thing, but that donation reaped a lifetime of rewards for the kingdom of God.

Later, I was given a free college education by a wealthy aunt. At the time I appreciated her generosity, but never as much as I do now that I have experienced the expenses of putting two children of my own through college. I look forward to the day when I, in return, can financially assist a student with college expenses.

Throughout your life you probably have heard sermons about giving. You know that God judges our giving not on the amount, but on the attitude with which we give.

Too many of us forget we can give in ways other than dollars and cents. We have garages stored with what we consider useless junk, but which to the poor would seem priceless treasures. Our closets are filled to overflowing with clothing the children have outgrown. When we get tired of old dishes and other paraphernalia, we toss them into junk boxes and store them out of sight until we can get to the closest dumpster.

Try to think of some practical ways you can help others with what you discard. Take the old musty tent that sleeps four, scrub it down with bleach, and then set it up in the sun for a week to air out. An agency in your community that serves the homeless can pass it on to a family who would have to sleep out of doors regardless of the weather. Along with it you could toss in some clothing, dishes, soap and food.

When you clean out your bookshelves, take discarded books to your local library or to a senior citizen's center. I have given several boxes of religious books to a library and later found them on the shelves. Such a donation is an unusual but effective way of sharing the Good News of Christ.

Donations of old games and toys are welcomed by classroom teachers. Panic strikes the heart of a teacher when rain cancels recess, but with a stack of games in the room, children are delighted to spend 30 minutes inside.

Many needy charities conduct yearly garage sales. If you keep boxes on hand all year round, you can easily collect used merchandise to donate.

We are richly blessed. No matter what our personal financial situations, we must identify and follow scriptural principles in the use of our money.

5. Plan for the future. Through hard work and sacrifice, some of us are able to have a small savings account for emergencies. The wise woman encourages her husband to budget money for this purpose. Solomon knew the importance of savings, for he said in Proverbs, "The wise man saves for the future, but the foolish man spends whatever he gets. A sensible man watches for problems ahead and prepares to meet them. The simpleton never looks, and suffers the consequences."

In Genesis 41:33-36, the Lord told Joseph to save grain during the seven years of plenteous crops. By doing so, he was able to provide food for Egypt and surrounding countries during the famine.

In Proverbs 6:6-8, the ant is referred to as a good example of working hard and storing up for lean months. The people of God are commanded to do the same thing.

By saving, we can know that our families will be provided for even after our death. According to Proverbs 13:22, it is our responsibility to do so: "A good man leaves an inheritance for his children's children, but a sinner's wealth is stored up for the righteous."

Spending money brings most women great pleasure, but the wise woman takes a serious look at her obligation to forego present enjoyment in order to provide for future contingencies.

How are you using your riches? Does your stewardship reflect your Christianity?

Lesson Three

Questions

1. With millions of people in the world going to bed hungry every night, is it wrong to salt away money in savings and investments?
2. If you have more money than you need for daily expenses, shouldn't you give it away?
3. How much would you need in savings if you or your husband were to be out of work for six months? (Financial experts say you should have at least six-months pay in savings should an emergency arise.)

4. Discuss the lesson about investing found in Luke 19:12-26.
5. Does God expect growth in what He entrusts to us? See Luke 19.

More wisdom for your meditation from the words of Solomon: Proverbs 3:27, 28; 11:24-26; 18:16; 19:17; 21:13; 22:9; 28:27.

Lesson Four

In Pursuit of Possessions

Sandra Humphrey, in *Christian Woman* magazine, gave the results of a survey taken 100 years ago, revealing that people had 72 "wants," 16 of which were considered "necessities." That survey, which had been repeated recently, stated that the average person now has 484 wants, 94 of which are considered absolute necessities.[1]

How long is your list of wants?

Advertisers would have us believe that material things bring happiness. If the first thing we purchase doesn't bring that satisfaction, then we go back and buy something that costs even more, sure that it's just what we need.

Jesus warned us about such behavior in Luke 12:15 when he said, "Watch out! Be on your guard against all kinds of greed; a man's life does not consist in the abundance of his possessions."

An ad in the "Lifestyles" section of *Newsweek* magazine mentioned a craze for $150 belt buckles and $695 rattlesnake belts. The Oprah

Winfrey television talk show once featured shop-aholics, and the camera revealed the closet contents of several women. One had 100 sweaters stacked neatly on shelves; another had 100 pairs of shoes and several racks of designer dresses. Both women revealed that they wore only 10 percent of the clothing they owned.

If having possessions is where we are finding true happiness, is it any wonder that Jesus said it would be more difficult for a rich man to enter heaven than for a camel to go through the eye of a needle (Matthew 19:24).

Recently I went to a Parade of Homes in Nashville. Picture, if you can, 10 luxurious homes valued between $250,000 and $400,000. They had *everything*, from double jacuzzis in the bedrooms to elegantly decorated exercise rooms on every level. The bathrooms were large enough to house entire families. Some had two bathtubs with two adjoining showers. One silk flower arrangement alone cost more than I spend on food for a family of four for a week.

I felt uncomfortable, as if through peeking into such an extravagant life-style, I was condoning the "building of better homes."

Did I feel a bit envious? Of course. My eye, finely tuned to aesthetic beauty, was extremely impressed with the interior design and the luxurious furniture. But in order to obtain such a home, I would have to amass a great fortune, which would take great time and energy and, most likely, a ruthless drive. I would have to spend endless numbers of hours decorating. Then the cleaning of such a home would undoubtedly require a full-time maid.

Would my impressive home be worth the effort? Would I be like many men and women who have struggled through years of work for such possessions and now are so fatigued that they've become couch potatoes, caring about nothing but evenings of rest at home in front of the television set? Where would my Lord fit into this world of materialism?

How Materialistic Are You?

Materialism can be thought of as the point you reach when you think something you own will make you happier, more successful, or more socially acceptable to others.

I once heard it expressed so beautifully: "You only go around once; so, stack up all the toys you can the first time!"

In the 1988 March/April issue of *Christian Woman*, Rachel Solomon defined materialism as "self-indulgence" and stated that most people can fight it only through sheer discipline, or like most of us, through limitation of income. She suggested honest self-appraisal of motivation and spending habits.[2] Such evaluations are of extreme worth as we attempt to be good stewards of our wealth.

Help for the Shopaholic

Last year at Christmas I received a teddy bear from one of my third-graders. Imprinted on its T-shirt were the words, "Born to shop." We all know people (mostly women) who would rather shop than eat. Merchants in this country encourage such behavior. More than 25,000 malls can be found in the United States—more than hospitals or school districts.

The shopaholic is one caught up in the trap of materialism. The person can often have a serious psychological problem, much like the alcoholic or drug-dependent person. Shopping becomes an obsession. Spending is out of control. The shopaholic shops to experience a "high," or she uses shopping as a tranquilizer. After all, a new dress *can* chase away a week of blues.

The shopaholic is not content with one item but goes on a buying binge, throwing caution to the wind for momentary pleasure. Such shopping usually results in unneeded purchases. Payment is often on credit, for the shopaholic has no concern for the future. Credit card companies are more than willing to give extended time to pay, a policy which only encourages the shopper to continue buying.

On "The Oprah Winfrey Show," audience participants told about hiding purchases from their spouses in order to avoid a confrontation.

If you think you might be a "shopaholic", ask yourself the following questions:

1. Is my closet filled with clothes I seldom wear?
2. Do I think that certain purchases are necessary for my well-being?
3. Do I shop on a regular basis? Monthly? Weekly? Do I think I have to shop in order to be happy?
4. Do I have more clothes to dress the body than books to dress the soul?
5. Do I allow myself to be influenced by advertising—the promise that my life will be better, that my popularity will increase, or that I'll be prettier?
6. Could I go one, two, or even three months without purchasing anything except the necessities of life?
7. Is my family doing without necessities because of my sporadic spending sprees?

If you answered "yes" to any of these questions, try charting your "Shouldn't Have Bought" purchases for a few weeks. Record these facts:

1. the circumstances under which the purchase was made

2. when you made it
3. who you were with
4. why you were in the store

Perhaps you spent the most after an argument with your husband or after a stressful week at work. Shopping is definitely a stress reducer, until the bills have to be paid! Once you see a pattern of spending, you can develop a workable plan for avoiding temptation.

I don't consider myself a shopaholic, but, like many people, I have often yielded to the temptation to purchase unnecessary items. I find it extremely difficult to resist country decor. And when I find a petite dress that fits, I simply can't turn it down. Such shopping has come to a screeching halt this year, for college expenses forbid such frivolities. I've had to make a definite plan to avoid temptation. The following are some suggestions I have found to be useful:

1. Plan alternative activities in times of stress, such as an evening out with friends or a good home video.

2. When you shop, predetermine how much you will spend. Leave your checkbook and charge cards at home, taking only cash.

3. Check with your mate before making any large purchase. Unless both of you can agree about its necessity, don't buy it.

4. Avoid shopping centers! This one simple

strategy has saved me an enormous amount of money in the last six months.

5. Psyche yourself into thinking you are too tired after a hard day's work to go shopping.

6. Pray. Our God is not too small to help with something as important as the stewardship of our blessings.

How can we become wiser shoppers, using our financial means to bring pleasure without overspending?

Rachel Solomon, in her article, suggests several questions you might ask yourself to avoid making an unnecessary purchase.[3]

1. *Is it a fad?* Scarves and other fashion accessories are beautiful, but prices are extremely high. Can I get more than one season's wear out of such a purchase?

2. *Will it serve several purposes?* Can a jacket be worn with slacks as well as skirts? Can I wear a belt with several outfits? Can I bring the patio furniture indoors for use in the rec room during winter months?

3. *Will it last?* Is the material durable or so flimsy that one could shoot a broomstraw through it? If it's furniture, is it well constructed? Will the jewelry bought on sale be tarnished by next year?

4. *Is it a necessary purchase or one to enhance my life or increase my acceptability?*

Have I bought it for its usefulness or for its status?

Be practical. The black silk dress is lovely for a special occasion, but how many other times during the course of a year can I wear it? The $50-a-plate china is exquisite, but won't food taste just as good on moderately priced Noritake?

5. *Is it worth what I have given up (e.g., a week's salary for a winter coat) to purchase it?*

To separate oneself from the materialistic pleasures of this life is difficult. Shopping is fun. I enjoy owning beautiful things, but I must shun any habits that distract me from the main goal in my life. I desire to live with the character of Jesus present in all circumstances. I want to live for Him here on this earth so that, when the final judgment arrives, I can appear before the throne of God free of spot or blemish, uncorrupted by the materialistic things of this world.

Remember, success is not in prosperity here, but prosperity there! "Set your mind on things above, not on earthly things" (Colossians 3:2).

Lesson Four

Questions

1. How much time do you spend taking care of what you own?
2. How do you feel around those who might be called *wealthy*?
3. Name some advertisements that have a tendency to make you feel discontented.
4. If you were given $1 million, what would you do with it?
5. Define *materialism*.
6. Tell about a time you bought something and later decided it wasn't what you wanted.

Notes Lesson Four

[1]Sandra Humphrey, "Sincerely Yours," *Christian Woman*, March-April 1988.

[2]Rachel Solomon, "Consumer or Consumed?," *Christian Woman*, March-April 1988.

[3]Ibid.

Lesson Five

In Pursuit of Success

This summer my 25-year high-school reunion will be held. I can't attend, but I've spent some time daydreaming about the people I would see and what they would be like now. I wonder how many I would recognize. Would I feel smug if some of my old girlfriends had more wrinkles and gray hair than I do? Would I secretly scan each face and body, seeing if I had retained my youth while others had gotten baggy and saggy?

How many will be on second, third, and maybe fourth husbands? How many have amassed great fortunes? How many have failed? Who's been the most successful? More important than my judgments of *them*, have *I* succeeded?

Mike Cope, in *Living in Two Worlds*, calls success our national battle cry. He says:

> "We eat it, breathe it, caress it, baby it, and even worse, judge ourselves by it. If we think we've lived up to society's stan-

dards for success, we're a success. Our ego is in good shape. We feel good about ourselves, so we treat others well. But if we don't think society sees us as a success, we think we've missed our calling."[1]

A few years ago we took a trip to the mountains of East Tennessee and spent several hours walking quietly through an eighteenth century graveyard. We were quiet and thoughtful, reminded that life is brief between the two dates etched on the tombstones of yesterday. What lies between those years? What lives on beyond the grave? Just what is this thing called success?

The world might see success as one or more of these:

- achievements
- physical appearance
- education
- abilities
- economic position
- marriage

Webster, in the *New World Dictionary, College Edition*, defines success as the "gaining of wealth, favor or eminence."

As Christians, we should be interested in God's view of success, not man's. True success lies not in wealth, fame or power, but in the contributions you have made to the world in which you live.

God's View of Success

How does God view success? Perhaps He sees the successful woman as one who follows these guidelines listed below.

1. *She seeks new goals and strives to reach them.* Spend a few hours every six months or so going over goals and expectations. What do you want out of life? How do you plan to achieve those things? Where is God on your list?

I never realized the importance of this assessment until several years ago. I was visiting with a friend who is a sales director for a national cosmetics network. Her company places individual goal-setting as a high priority. In the course of our conversation, Mary asked me what my goal for the year was. I fumbled for words, trying to come up with an intelligent answer. After receiving a much-needed lecture on the value of setting goals and priorities, I went home that very day and wrote in my journal a list of objectives for the year. Under each I listed activities that would bring about the achievement of the goal. I established a time frame in which to work.

In the coming year, I periodically reviewed my list and prayed that God would guide and bless me in my endeavors. I knew that only by surrendering my plans and activities to a God who knows what is best for my life would I succeed:

> "Commit thy way unto the Lord; trust also in him; and he shall bring it to pass" (Psalm 37:5).

> "Trust in the Lord with all thine heart, and lean not unto thine own understanding. In all thy ways acknowledge Him, and He shall direct thy paths" (Proverbs 3:5, 6).

Goal setting is now a part of my life. I would never attempt to write a book or undertake any other major project without committing it to thoughtful planning and prayer, allowing God to work through me to accomplish each and every goal.

When we cease trying to make self the supreme architect and let God do the planning, life assumes the right direction and purpose.

2. *She gives herself totally to God.* In public worship and in quiet times, she practices His presence in every moment of the day, turning over all decisions to His wisdom. *Spiritual Aerobics* was filled with suggestions about how to be a self-disciplined person devoted to a spiritual lifestyle. Walking with God consists of more than warming a church pew three times a week. I confess that's what I have done for

months on end. My spiritual life has been like a yo-yo, never resting in the same spot for any length of time.

Only through dedicated, regular soul searching and prayer can I bring my spiritual life into proper focus. Scarcely a day goes by that I am not faced with a new task, a new challenge, or a new opportunity. Many seem beyond my capabilities, but when I let God take over and furnish the strength and direction while I supply the trust and willingness, I can turn obstacles into opportunities and accomplish great things.

3. *She makes her life count for eternity.* She pursues activities that have a long-lasting, far-reaching effect in the kingdom of God.

In an earlier chapter, I mentioned deeds done for me as a child that had far-reaching effects on my life and those people whose lives I touch every day. I am reminded of Hebrews 11:6: ". . . God spoke well of his [Abel] offerings. And by faith he still speaks, even though he is dead."

Though many of the people who poured gifts of love into my life are now gone, their gifts and encouragement still speak through my deeds. These are the far-reaching effects of a life that counts for eternity.

In Chapter 6, we will study the different ways our bodies are used to glorify God. Through the wise use of our talents and abilities, we can make every activity give praise and honor to the

God who created us. Praising Him with our lives is the true success.

4. *She does her very best at all times.* She responds to life's challenges with personal growth and commitment.

I commend those who do office work. They must have patience, be dedicated to detail, and have possession of secretarial skills. I discovered that such talent lies outside the realm of my own abilities.

A few summers ago, I worked in a medical office, spending most of my day filing, answering the telephone, and performing other tasks which were simply not to my liking. I found myself dreading the days that stretched out before me.

One verse kept coming to mind: "Whatever your hand finds to do, do it with all your might . . ." (Ecclesiastes 9:10).

The verse calls me to tackle every task with determination and zeal, to not be slothful or half-hearted about my work. I have to lay aside personal preferences, likes and dislikes, and be willing to perform those things which might be distasteful to me. If I must bag groceries, I will do it with a smile on my face. If my job calls for me to type 100 pages a day, I will type that many plus 10 more if there's time. If my talent is in the teaching profession, I will be dedicated to that field. Everything I do will present a

challenge to be met with growth and commitment. Only then will I experience success as
God measures it.

5. *She finds her gifts.* She trusts in the qualities of those gifts and their contributions to the
world and their value. She is "confident that
He who has begun a good work in you will
complete it until the day of Jesus Christ" (Philippians 1:6).

God has created a work in each of us, and
as stewards of His blessings, we are to search
for our talents and create opportunities to succeed within the radius of those abilities and
gifts. If I love children, I look for opportunities
to teach or care for them. If I write, I look for
opportunities to publish that others might benefit from that talent. If I am a good listener, I
make myself available for those who need to
talk. Everything that I do reflects the talents
with which I have been blessed, that I might
"complete it until the day of Jesus Christ."

6. *She recognizes her weaknesses and copes
with them while striving to improve.* If I am to
be a successful woman, I must look for those
areas of life in which I need improvement.
That's not a difficult thing to do for most of us.
Each day I find another weakness in myself. It
might be my inability to refuse rich, fatty des-
serts or my inability to stick to a task. Once I
am aware of my weakness, I ask God for strength

to overcome so that I might give full attention to those things that are of true importance in life.

7. *She sees herself as a person of worth.* Our feelings of self-esteem and worth are tied in with childhood experiences, teen relationships, college, marriage, job, family and friends. It can take years to overcome negative influences. We also must realize that success is not tied in any way to fame, wealth or worldly beauty but to our relationship to God and family.

How sad it would be to face eternity knowing that you have wasted your life—no souls won, no spiritual gifts exercised for fruit, no ministry to the poor. "What does it profit a man, if he gain the whole world, and lose his soul" (Matthew 16:26)?

Woodrow Wilson once said it this way:

> No man ever came to the end of his life, and had time and a little space of calm from which to look back upon it, who did not know and acknowledge that it was what he had done unselfishly for others, and nothing else, that satisfied him and made him feel that he had played the man. And so we grow by having responsibility placed upon us, the burden of other people's business.

Man's view of success is how high we climb.

God's view of success is where we started and where we ended.

No matter what our position in life, all of us can be successful in His sight and can hear Him say, "Well done, thy good and faithful servant" (Matthew 25:21).

Lesson Five

Questions

1. How do you handle success? Study the following verses: 1 Corinthians 4:7; Philippians 2:3.
2. In Jeremiah 9:23 we are given detailed instructions for acquiring a humble spirit. What attitude should we have toward success as spoken of by the prophet?
3. True success in the end is an eternal home in heaven. What characteristics do we need to portray in order to receive that reward as given in Psalm 15?
4. What are some ways a woman can destroy a home by her desire for success?
5. Role-play an office situation in which two women are trying to move up the ladder of success in a company through un-Christlike tactics.

Notes Lesson Five

[1]Mike Cope, *Living in Two Worlds*, (Nashville: Gospel Advocate, 1987), p. 21.

Lesson Six

In Pursuit of Youth and Beauty

The first thing I have to look at every morning is a face that makes me want to groan aloud! The white hairs sprinkled among the black stand up and beg to be noticed. Creases from the pillow slip have made caverns in my cheeks. The wrinkles around my eyes stand out like road maps. I lather on gooey cream to bring this aging skin back to life and later apply makeup to camouflage the caverns and wrinkles. Each time I go to the hairdresser, I anxiously ask, "Is it time for me to try to cover up the gray?"

I have to admit it. I'm getting older, and with the aging of my body comes the aging of my skin and hair. Do I accept it and do the best with what I have, or do I plunge ahead full speed into another trivial pursuit, constantly striving to fight the inevitable, spending a mild fortune on wrinkle creams and anti-aging formulas that promise miracles?

Brainwashed into thinking we are acceptable only if we are beautiful, we constantly strive for that "young, fresh" look.

In past years, I've attended parties that taught me what colors I should wear to bring out my "beautiful" features. I've learned how to apply makeup to cover flaws and enhance good features. I've learned what styles of clothing I should wear to accentuate the good and camouflage the bad. I've pounded the pavement, sweated at the gym, and starved myself to be thin. Most of you have joined me in contributing to the billions of dollars being poured into the makeup industry.

Then, if it's still not good enough, we can have a facelift, have a tummy tuck, or even have some of that fat "sucked" away in liposuction surgery. A plastic surgeon would say, "If you don't like what you have, add to it or take it away!"

Let's face it; we're all vain. I'm not a Miss America, but I confess that I work hard at trying to do the best with what I have. Why? Because it makes me feel better. I believe I am more credible as a writer, speaker, teacher, minister's wife and even mother if I am neat and well groomed.

If you invited me to speak in a seminar, and I appeared in crumpled clothing and tennis shoes and had disheveled hair and a dirty face, would you listen to what I had to say?

Grooming and exercise are all part of the daily self-disciplining activities that make up a part of the total "me." As in all areas of life, though, I can become over concerned—even obsessed—with my appearance.

Ask yourself the following questions. Your answers will help you determine your motivation for your personal grooming activities.

1. Do I spend more time applying make-up and working on my wardrobe each day than I spend in Bible study and prayer?

2. Do I spend more money on grooming expenditures than I give to the Lord?

3. Do I take money from the family budget that could be used for more necessary items?

4. Have I fallen prey to false advertising claims for products to remove wrinkles or make me more attractive in some way?

5. Do I spend a large portion of my grooming time anxiously searching for wrinkles and white hairs?

6. Will I suffer depression when I hit the middle years and signs of aging appear?

If you answered "yes" to more than two of these questions, chances are you need to take another look at your priorities.

I have always, even from my youth, disliked the appearance of my hands. The knuckles wrinkle, my fingers are too short, and the nails just won't grow! After I read the following story, I began to question my anxiety.

> On the grounds of a royal palace grew a garden of breathtaking beauty. This garden was cared for by three beautiful maidens.
>
> In the middle of the garden were sparkling streams and fragrant roses—more beautiful than the eye could imagine.
>
> Legend tells us that one day there arose a discussion as to which of the three maids had the most beautiful hands.
>
> Eleanor, who had tinted her white fingers while gathering strawberries, vowed that hers were the most beautiful. Antoinette had been pruning and caring for the roses, and she thought hers the most lovely. The other sister, Joan, had been dipping her fingers in the clear stream and the drops of water were sparkling like diamonds on her tapered fingers. She thought her hands were the most beautiful.
>
> As they were arguing, a beggar came to the garden gate begging for alms. The three sisters turned away in disgust, pulling their rich, elegant robes about them.
>
> She went on down the path and came to a nearby cottage. There she met an old woman with a sun-burned face and hands that showed marks of many years of toil

and strain. In that cottage the beggar was
given food and lovingly cared for.

Legend states that the beggar was in-
stantly transformed into an angel who
returned to the palace gate saying, "The
most beautiful hands are those which are
found ready to bless and help their fellowman."[1]

Does your body glorify God? Have you become
so concerned with beauty that you have failed
to use your hands for God's service? As we grow
older our skin looks wrinkled, and our hands
often resemble the hide of an alligator. But no
matter how old or how ugly, the touch is the
same when given in love.

As we become more and more concerned
with outward beauty, we tend to forget the real
reason we have been placed on planet earth—to
serve others, as Christ served us.

A Godly Look at Beauty and Youthfulness

What's really important? Is it wrong to be
concerned over appearance? How much is too
much?

I believe it is important . . .

1. . . . that the people in my life aren't ashamed
    of the way I look.

2. . . . that I eat those foods that maintain good health and avoid those foods that damage my physical well-being.

3. . . . that I exercise daily in order to be physically fit.

4. . . . that I am not any heavier than I should be.

5. . . . that my dress reflect my Christianity.

6. . . . that I accept my flaws, imperfections, and the signs of aging that are all in the plan of God and to do the best with what I have.

7. . . . that I reflect the glory of God through "inner" beauty.

Ralph Waldo Emerson once said, "There is no beautifier of complexion, or form, or behavior, like the wish to scatter joy and not pain around us."

Charles Dickens agreed when he wrote, "Cheerfulness and contentment are great beautifiers and are famous preservers of youthful looks."

Upon Aging

Why do we dread getting old? Victor Hugo said it this way:

Winter is on my head, but eternal spring is in my heart; I breathe at this hour the

fragrance of the lilacs, the violets, and the
roses, as at twenty years ago. The nearer
I approach to the end, the plainer I hear
around me the immortal symphoniers of
the world which invite me.

What is your attitude toward aging? Are you
planning now for that time in which you will
be free from so many of the responsibilities that
tie you down to a time when you will be able
to be of even greater service to God?

Are you afraid of the empty nest, dreading
the quiet empty house without the sounds of
children? Do you realize that this period can
be a time for adding new dimensions to your
life?

Life with my children has been rich and full.
I have never regretted a moment. The children
are in college now (in the same town, but living
in the dormitory). Next year one of them will
attend a college 1,000 miles away. I feel great
pain when I think of my empty nest. Yet, at the
same time, I look forward to having time to do
the thousands of things I want to do. The period
will just be another stage in this performance
of life. I'm reminded of Solomon's words in
Ecclesiastes 3: "There is a time for everything . . . ."

When I can accept that and know there is a
time to live with the wrinkles, a time to enjoy

the sheen of silver hair, a time to slow down my pace, and a time to accept the silent still house which once echoed with the sounds of children's laughter, then I, too, will have the wisdom of Solomon, and I'll possess an inward beauty that the years cannot take away.

You have unique, special qualities that make you the individual you are. God has given you the potential to develop into an even more creative, vibrant and fit person, regardless of the fragile shell in which you live. Get busy!

Lesson Six

Questions

1. If you could look like any other person, who would you choose? Why?
2. Share with the class one thing that bothers you about your appearance.
3. Discuss feelings concerning makeup parties and style shows.
4. Discuss some ways of dealing with the empty-nest syndrome.
5. Discuss the crisis men and women go through when entering middle age. What role should the church play in helping those experiencing such a crisis?

Notes Lesson Six

[1]Mrs. Charles Cowman, *Streams in the Desert,* Vol. 2 (Grand Rapids: Zondervan, 1966).

Lesson Seven

In Search of Sensuality

We live in a sex-oriented society. Our society pursues cheap thrills through illicit and immoral sexual activities. Almost every drama or sitcom on television contains explicit sex or treats it with distasteful humor. Pornographic "sex" houses can be found in every major city, and family bookstores peddle pornography under the heading "eroticism."

Never has the challenge against purity been stronger. Forces more powerful than any we can imagine are at work to erode a once pure and proud nation.

Dial-A-Porn

A $2.4 billion industry, dial-a-porn is targeted for adults but is snowballing into addictive behavior for young children. By just pushing a few buttons on the telephone, one can get a recorded message or an intimate conversation about anything from "simple" obscene "talk" to directions about how to commit a rape.

In one state a young boy molested a child and later confessed that he had been making up to 50 calls a day to a sex number. In another case, a 10-year-old boy was raped by two teens who had been using the Dial-A-Sex number.

Dial-a-porn was intended for adult use, and used it has been. The *Chattanooga News-Free Press* published an article revealing that the Defense Department long-distance telephone calls sheet revealed $25,000 in monthly charges for Pentagon calls to dial-a-porn services.

In the summer of 1988, thanks to activist groups, Congress passed a law banning obscene and indecent dial-a-porn. However, that law is unenforceable. Pornographers have challenged the law twice, stating that not all pornography is obscene; therefore, not all dial-a-porn is unlawful. Major flaws exist in the current bill, and as long as these flaws remain unchallenged, the people in the dial-a-porn industry will remain virtually immune from federal prosecution.

Citizen action is probably the most effective way to stop dial-a-porn. At the end of this chapter, you will find suggestions to help fight this disturbing element of our society. The fight is going to be nasty, for some people are determined to keep the industry going—in spite of the facts that our children are being violated, that once a child calls, he quickly becomes addicted to such messages, and that dial-a-porn contributes to a sex-crazed society.

The United States needs Christians to take a stand.

The Music Industry

When I was a teen-ager, the thing most disturbing to the older generation in my home was the pounding beat of rock music. Today's parents have a more serious concern; rock music lyrics focus on drug abuse, suicide, sex, incest and rape. When a vulnerable teen-ager listens to hours a day of lyrics proposing un-Christian and even Satanic sexual activities, parents have a right to be concerned. We as parents can't monitor every song played on rock radio stations, but we can fight for legislation to put an end to such ungodly influence on our children. (This subject will be discussed in detail in Chapter 8.)

Homosexuality

Now accepted as a part of society, practicing homosexuals have formed activist groups and demand to be heard in every area of life, from teaching to the ministry.

Movies

We're no longer shocked by anything shown on the silver screen. Sex is an acceptable part of any prime-time movie or sitcom. We are conditioned to what we see, rather than outraged by it.

Advertising

Sex is used to sell everything. Just watch your television for one evening and chart the number of times sex is used to sell a product.

Adultery

The promise to "love and cherish, until death do us part" has become obsolete. Immoral behavior is modeled to the American public 24 hours a day. The norm is to leave your husband or wife for another.

Lest you believe that as a Christian woman you are immune to such temptation, ask any minister or Christian counselor to give you statistics concerning adulterous relationships in the church. In every congregation numerous lives have been shattered by the "other" man or woman.

How does a Christian become sexually involved with another partner? Richard Exley, in *The Rhythm of Life*, states:

> I am convinced that more people get themselves into the pain of infidelity through empathy, concern and compassion than through any base motive. The world is full of lonely and vulnerable people, hungry for a sympathetic ear and a shoulder to cry on. With a little help from rationalization, the sympathy leads smoothly into tenderness, the tenderness to the need for privacy, the privacy to physical consolation, and the consolation straight to bed.[1]

Many women fall into the pit of adultery because emotional needs are not met at home. In the book *Affair Prevention*, Peter Kereitler and Bill Bruns concur:

> Affairs begin not just for sexual reasons but to satisfy the basic need we all have for closeness, goodness, kindness, togetherness. . . . When these needs are not met on a regular basis in a marriage, the motivations may be to find a person who will be good to us, touch us, hold us, give us a feeling of closeness. Sexual fulfillment may indeed become an important part of an extramarital relationship, but the "ness"

needs, are for most men and women I
know, initially more important.[2]

God made the nature of woman different from
man. Men find it difficult to understand our
need for touch, warmth and emotional security.
So, when someone pays us a little attention, the
mind can begin to play dangerous tricks.

As I talked with one fine Christian lady, a
deacon's wife, who found herself enmeshed in
such a situation, she related the following story:

> The days and nights were agony. I knew
> that what I was feeling was wrong. I
> couldn't eat. I couldn't sleep. I experi-
> enced actual pain in the chest area.
>
> Here was a man who had been a dear
> friend, who shared my deepest thoughts
> and feelings, on a friendship level. Then,
> all of a sudden, the physical began, totally
> unexpected. We both knew what had to
> be done and spent many hours on our
> knees praying for strength and wisdom.
> Never have I prayed more earnestly.
>
> Those hours in prayer gave us both the
> strength to separate ourselves from one
> another emotionally, and the wisdom to
> remove ourselves physically from any temp-
> tation that came our way. The opportunity
> came for my husband to accept a job
> transfer to another city, and I knew that
> God had answered my prayer in the best
> possible way.

And you think it couldn't happen to you?

> Therefore do not let sin reign in your mortal bodies, so that you obey its evil desires. Do not offer the parts of your body to sin, as instruments of wickedness, but rather offer yourselves to God, as those who have been brought from death to life, and offer the parts of your body to him as instruments of righteousness (Romans 6:12, 13).

God's people are called to a holy life-style, one free from deeds of the flesh. His will is for us to deny the lusts of the flesh which daily surround us.

> It is God's will that you should be sanctified: that you should avoid sexual immorality; that each of you should learn to control his own body in a way that is holy and honorable; not in passionate lust like the heathen, who do not know God; and that in this matter no one should wrong his brother or take advantage of him. The Lord will punish men for all such sins, as we have already told you and warned you. For God did not call us to be impure, but to live a holy life. Therefore he who rejects this instruction does not reject man but God, who gives you his Holy Spirit (1 Thessalonians 4: 3-8).

Adultery *is* a sin. Purity *is* achievable. God gives us much help to overcome through His Word. We're not weak puppets when we are confronted with the temptation to be unfaithful, to read a smutty magazine, or to watch an unfit movie. Through Christ we can win the victory.

> For the grace of God which brings salvation has appeared to all men. It teaches us to say no to ungodliness and worldly passions, and to live self-controlled, upright and godly lives in this present age, while we wait for the blessed hope—the glorious appearing of our great God and Savior Jesus Christ, who gave himself for us to redeem us from all wickedness and to purify for himself a people that are his very own, eager to do what is good (Titus 2:11-14).

The battle is on! You, with the help of God, can resist the sexual temptations of an X-rated society.

1. *Avoid tempting situations.* In other words, run! If you know that being around a certain man causes you to have a desire that is unlawful in God's sight, remove yourself from that situation, even if it means quitting a job.

2. *Don't feed on lustful material.* It's everywhere—in grocery stores, in bookstores, and on television. Stay away from it. More adulterous

sex takes place on daily soap operas than on prime-time television. How can we be rooting for these shows and still say we have a heart with God?

3. *Remember you are a Christian and that you have been put here for a purpose.* Your purpose is to glorify God and worship Him with your body, not to dishonor it through immoral living.

4. *Turn your battle over to the Lord.* Drop to your knees when you are faced with temptation. God will provide a way of escape. He's promised it! "No temptation has seized you except what is common to man. And God is faithful; he will not let you be tempted beyond what you can bear. But when you are tempted he will also provide a way out so that you can stand up under it" (1 Corinthians 10:13 *NIV*).

5. *Get to know your own body.* What weakens your control of it? Do you know, or are you aware of, danger signals? Do you know when danger is approaching? Do you know how to stay clear of the danger zone? The following verses show you how.

> Therefore I urge you brothers, in view of God's mercy, to offer your bodies as living sacrifices, holy and pleasing to God— this is your spiritual act of worship. Do not conform any longer to the pattern of

the world, but be transformed by the re-
newing of your mind. Then you will be
able to test and approve what God's will
is—his good, pleasing, and perfect will
(Romans 12:1, 2).

To the world, sex is in! To the Christian, sex
is a pursuit that can lead to a broken life and
the loss of that final crown of righteousness.
"Be thou faithful unto death, and I will give
thee a crown of life" (Revelation 2:10).

Lesson Seven

Questions

1. State your definition of purity.
2. Can a person recover purity after backsliding?
3. Read 1 Thessalonians 4:1-8. List three reasons
   we need to be pure.
4. What do the following verses teach about avoiding temptation? 1 Corinthians 6:18; 1 Peter 5:8;
   1 Corinthians 6:12-20; 1 Thessalonians 4:4.
5. In Colossians 3:17 we are told to do all things
   in the name of the Lord. Name some areas in
   the realm of sensuality in which you could use
   this verse as an ally against the devil.
6. How do we respond when a brother or sister
   slides into immorality? Read Galatians 6:1, 2;
   James 5:19, 20; Matthew 18:15-17.

7. Read Galatians 5:13,16, 17. List the deeds of the flesh.
8. Role-play the following situation: After a close friend finds herself in a situation in which she is attracted to someone outside the marriage bond, she comes to you for advice. What would you tell her?
9. What is a woman to do when her mate does not give her the emotional ties and fulfillment needed in her life? Offer *concrete* suggestions.
10. What are some typical situations in which a woman might become attracted to a man other than her husband?
11. Discuss the dangers of allowing children to watch R-rated movies on cable television.
12. How would you react if a man who worked with you began making friendly overtures? What if you found yourself enjoying these advances?
13. Can a Christian man and woman who are married to others share a friendship?

Activities

The following are activities and addresses of interest to those concerned about the dial-a-porn industry. Suggestions are taken from the *Focus on the Family Citizen* newsletter (Summer, 1988).

1. Put pressure on your local phone company if it still carries dial-a-porn. The law is on the side of the phone company if it is truly interested in disconnecting phone sex.

2. Write your congresspersons and senators, asking them to support legislation that makes the transmission of obscene dial-a-porn a felony with stiff fines and prison sentences.

3. Encourage U.S. attorneys in their efforts to prosecute pornographers. Make your letters positive and affirming.

4. Subscribe to *The Obscenity Enforcement Reporter,* published by the National Obscenity Enforcement Unit, Criminal Division, Department of Justice, Room 2216, 10th and Constitution Ave., NW, Washington, D.C. 20530. A one-year subscription is $5 for six issues. (Suggestion: send in one subscription for the entire class and review each issue together).

5. Get involved in an antipornography group. Write to the following groups:

American Family Association
P.O. Drawer 2440
Tupelo, MS 38803

Morality in Media
475 Riverside Drive
New York, NY 10115

National Coalition Against Pornography
800 Compton Road
Suite 9224
Cincinnati, OH 45231

Notes Lesson Seven

[1]Richard Exley, *The Rhythm of Life* (Tulsa: Harrison House, 1987) p. 30.

[2]Peter Kereitler and Bill Bruns, *Affair Prevention* (New York, MacMillan, 1981) p. 74.

Lesson Eight

Where Have All the Children Gone?

After more than a decade, my memories of the characters in the first-grade reader are still fresh. I can visualize Dick and Jane in yellow raincoats and black galoshes, splashing through rain puddles shouting,

"Look, Dick, look!
See, Jane.
See the rain!"

Today's first-grade basal text might read:

"Get up, Sally.
Get up.
Hurry, hurry.
Mother works.
Father works.
You must go to day-care today.
Hurry, Sally.
Hurry."

The "hurried child" described so accurately by David Elkind in his popular book by that name could aptly be renamed the "extinct" child. Elkind writes,

> Hurried children are forced to take on the physical, psychological, and social trappings of adulthood before they are prepared to deal with them. We dress our children in miniature adult costumes (often with designer labels), we expose them to gratuitous sex and violence, and we expect them to cope with an increasingly bewildering social environment. . . . Through all of these pressures the child senses that it is important for him or her to cope without admitting the confusions and pain that accompany such changes. Like adults, they are made to feel that they must be survivors, and surviving means adjusting—even if the survivor is only four or six or eight years old.[1]

Our hurried children have become the unwilling victims of a sinful culture. We parents have become so caught up in the stresses of daily living that we no longer realize that our world is untrustworthy. Our world sends out conflicting messages to its children.

While American moms and dads are marching daily to the beat of the work-world drum, they are unknowingly placing on their children an enormous overload of responsibility, and the results can be disastrous.

Children: The Vanishing Species

Where *have* all the children gone? is a question I ask each fall as I open the doors of my classroom to 25 to 30 elementary-aged youngsters. I've watched the change evolve over the last decade. Where has their innocence gone? What's hiding beneath the tough exterior of the child of this century? Have we been so busy pursuing dreams of personal wealth and success that we've forgotten the children, leaving them behind to fend for themselves in a world that seeks to exploit and manipulate its young?

God's in His heaven, but all is not right with our children. Unless our present society returns childhood to its rightful owners, we might as well begin the funeral dirge.

> The hazards of the adult world, sometimes fatal temptations, descend upon children so early that the ideal of childhood is demolished (Morrow, Lance. *Time*, Aug. 8, 1988).

Hi Ho, Hi Ho, It's Off to Work We Go . . .

Children have a right to childhood and its pleasures. Their activities should be fun and meant for children, not always performed for the purpose of perfecting skills and abilities or for the sake of competition. In past years we've transformed play into work. We send off our children each day as if they, like the seven dwarfs, were armed with pick and axe and singing,

> "Hi, ho, hi, ho.
> It's off to work
> we go. . . ."

And when they come home from their "work-day," we inundate their senses with blood, gore, sex and violence on television.

America's Favorite Baby-Sitter

As a teacher, I've watched children's taste in television programming and movies change from the innocence of "Alice in Wonderland" to the killings of hideous monsters carrying hatchets and chain saws and to the brandishing hands that carry fingers made of steel knives. Jason, the hideous killer in "Friday the 13th," is every child's closet monster.

Students in one Christian school, when asked to rate their favorite horror movies, put these at the top of the list:

"The Texas Chainsaw Massacre"
"Nightmare on Elm Street"
"My Bloody Valentine"
"Return of the Living Dead"
"Friday the 13th"

Children are fascinated with movies that depict actual death scenes. Our children no longer seem to be frightened by brutal and hideous violence.

Television portrays bizarre examples of reality, totally incomprehendable to the mind of a child. During one week of summer talk-show programming, children of America watched as transsexuals, homosexual ministers and prostitutes gave their promiscuous views of life, love, and the pursuit of happiness.

Because they are inundated with such knowledge, children begin sex and drug experimentation at an early age. Much of this experimentation occurs during those after-school hours while our children are left unsupervised.

Some studies suggest that everything we experience is recorded on our brain, never to be forgotten. Children who view slasher-horror films possibly will carry the memory of grisly murder scenes forever, unable to free themselves from unwanted memories.

In Colossians 3:12, Christians are instructed to "put on a heart of compassion, humility, gentleness, and patience." In verse 17, we are reminded that "whatever you do in word or deed, do all in the name of the Lord Jesus."

How will our children be able to have such pure hearts when such wicked scenes have entered the senses through the media? How can seeing such movies and shows be done in the name of Jesus?

Whatever Happened to Mom, Dad, and the Kids?

Many children come home to an empty house and to face excessive stress in the family unit. Only one in five families is traditional. The roles of father, mother and children have been rewritten. Divorce is socially acceptable. Some children live with one parent and visit another. Some live with two parents of the same sex (homosexuals) attempting to raise normal children. Society will bear the consequences of such behavior far into the future. In *Psychology Today*, Norval Glenn wrote, "One must seriously entertain the disturbing hypothesis that the increased number of children of divorce will lead to a slow but steady erosion of the population's overall level of well-being."[2]

In the Classroom

If all the information in this chapter sounds alarmingly negative, it's because I'm concerned. As a teacher I'm in a position to witness first-hand the damage done by the "hurrying" of today's child. I struggle to teach the basics to many children who have a poor attention span and a difficult time concentrating. Many students can't remain seated more than five minutes at a time. Schools in every county in the nation report behaviorally disoriented children of every age out of control, children who can't discipline themselves. Many are impulsive, can't obey the rules, show lack of responsibility, are truant, and use drugs and alcohol.

Dr. Marvin Watson, former president of Dallas Baptist University, did an enlightening comparison of major school offenses in 1940 and 1980. In 1940 the offenses were running in hallway, chewing gum, wearing improper clothing (T-shirts, untucked), making noises, and not putting paper in the wastebasket. In 1980 the problems were robbery-assaults, personal threats, burglary, drug abuse, carrying weapons, vandalism, murder and extortion.

Overall, the picture is pretty glum.

Joseph Novella, M.D., who wrote *Bringing Up Kids American Style,* speaks the truth about such children:

> Beneath the tough bravados beat frightened young hearts. These boys and girls fear their impulses and fear a world that cannot, or will not, help them to bring themselves under control. Their parents, too, are scared and intimidated. They have lost their position of leadership in the family. The kids, quite literally, are in charge.[3]

Where *have* all the children gone? Will Dick and Jane ever again represent the norm as they splash happily through the rain-soaked streets? Can we bring back the magical, dreamy qualities of childhood?

Lance Morrow, in *Time,* August, 1988, says, "Each childhood is distinctive, the first chapter of a new biography in the world, and its truth is in the individual details." In the classrooms of tomorrow, the children will be reading the biographies of the children of today. What details will emerge?

One Voice . . . Singing in the Darkness

Life in the fast lane is tough for our children. We can't tuck them away in a safe little corner of the world; their surroundings often will be negative and stressful. Neither can we isolate them from evil. We can't bear their pain or solve their problems. We can't do for them those things they dislike to do, such as study, take tests, or get a job.

But we *can* protect them from those forces that would steal from the children the precious years of childhood. We can allow them the freedom to enjoy all the good and beautiful things this life has to offer. We can make a commitment to provide healthful, creative opportunities for play and enjoyment. We can become one voice—a voice against the exploitation and manipulation of children—and we can make that voice heard across the country.

Lesson Eight Activities

Please take the time to discuss each issue facing the children of today.

Because this lesson is so relevant and its message so urgent, questions are omitted so the class might take the time to write letters of concern to those who attempt to rob our children of their rightful place in society.

Special thanks to the *Focus on the Family Citizen Paper* for the addresses and guidelines listed in "Rock Music" and "Television."

Rock Music

"Rising to the Challenge," a video strictly for adults, contains carefully documented evidence regarding the themes of rebellion, drug and alcohol abuse, explicit sex, the occult, and violence found in some of today's music. The video is produced by Teen Vision, a Pennsylvania-based Parents' Music Resource Center, and distributed by Spring Arbor Distributors, a Belleville, MI, wholesaler specializing in Christian books and videos. For more information, write—Teen Visions, Inc., 321 Third Ave., Carnegie, PA 15106.

Together with the National PTA and the American Academy of Pediatrics, the Parents' Music Resource Center is fighting for parents' rights to decide what is suitable listening material for their children. The Virginia-based organization aims specifically to identify albums containing lyrics that glamorize murder, rape, violence, suicide, drugs and alcohol, so parents might be aware of and monitor what their children listen to. Write Parents' Music Resource Center, 1500 Arlington Blvd., Arlington, VA 22209.

Request a petition that will tell music industry executives that parents do indeed want lyrics and labels on album covers.

Television

Networks don't cancel a show because of the language or the quality, but because of ratings.

To express your opinion of current programming, write to the following:

ABC
1330 Avenue of the Americas
New York, NY 10019

CBS
51 West 52 Street
New York, NY 10019

NBC
30 Rockefeller Plaza
New York, NY 10112

You may also write to the advertisers of the offensive program.

Notes Lesson Eight

[1]David Elkind, *The Hurried Child* (Reading: Addison-Wesley Pub. Co., 1981), p. 104.

[2]Norval Glenn, "Children of Divorce," *Psychology Today* (June, 1985).

[3]Joseph Novella, M.D., *Bringing Up Kids American Style* (New York: A. and W. Publishers, 1986), p. 115.

Lesson Nine

Removing
the Mask

I often find myself people-watching Sunday mornings between Bible study and worship. Sights and sounds of joyous fellowship fill the building and echo from the rafters. At first appearance, all who are present seem to be bubbling over with joy and happiness.

But, alas. All are not joyous. On the fourth row back, Janie is grieving over the death of her mother. The handsome gentleman in front of me has just discovered his wife has been unfaithful. The minister, cheerfully greeting members, has been dismissed and asked to leave in six weeks. Just last week the song leader learned he has cancer.

Each Christian appears on the surface to be well-contented with life. Each is wearing a mask—the same mask many of us don each morning before we face the world of work and play.

Such were the thoughts that inspired me to write the following lines several years ago:

Masks aren't just for ghouls and goblins at Halloween . . . they're for ordinary people playing a losing game of Hide-and-Seek with their fellowman.

My own masks (I have several in my daily wardrobe) are worn with use and are perfect fits. Each morning I clamp down the mask of my choice and screw it tightly into place. Then I make sure the others are in a convenient place, ready to grab at a moment's notice.

Today I might want to hide my insecurities and emotional struggles. Tomorrow my mask might cover a cold and apathetic spirit, a loneliness for the love of a friend, or a yearning to share the deepest secrets of my life.

On some days I will wear my "I'm tough" mask. On those days things are not going so well, but I don't want anyone to know that they're getting me down. I can handle anything, without help from anyone.

When I don't want anyone to bother me, I wear my "keep your distance" mask. It comes in handy when I just don't have the time to get involved. I really don't need any friends.

You see, I need these masks. If I take them off, I'm vulnerable. Others might see a mirror of their own pain on the surface of my suffering. They might feel a need to reach in and take some of my pain on themselves.

Then I wouldn't be "tough" anymore, and I would have to discard my "Keep your distance" mask.

Stripped bare of all my masks, I feel vulnerable, weak, needing the love and support of others.

Masks. We all wear them as part of our daily wardrobe. Why?

Isolationism

Never has the American society been so isolated from itself. We go to great lengths to keep others from knowing our pain and from having to share theirs.

If anyone tries to get too close, we simply slam shut the doors of our hearts and slap on the mask that fits the occasion.

We live in isolated "bubbles" for other reasons. Ours is a transient society. We move into a neighborhood and five years later move out again. To protect ourselves from the pain of separation, we have refrained from getting "close" to anyone. Neighbors living just feet from our own back door are virtual strangers!

When Do You Wear Your Mask?

Several things can cause us to don our masks:
- Fatigue
- Sickness and suffering
- Burnout
- Inner struggles and turmoil
- Sin

In some circumstances, a mask is necessary. It can shield others from our pain when pain is not appropriate. It can enable us to fulfill our responsibilities.

When a loved one is seriously ill, we hide behind the mask of cheerfulness and optimism in order to keep up that person's spirits. We put on a mask to hide feelings of grief or frustration when others are depending upon us, such as in teaching a class. We might put on a mask on Sunday morning, so others can be uplifted by our presence in the worship service.

Such acts are acts of unselfishness and compassion. We have put the feelings and expectations of others above our own.

We wear other masks to keep people at a distance—to remain uninvolved in their lives. These masks build walls that separate us from our fellowman. They keep us from being honest and open and accountable.

Open Relationships

Can you think of a time when you needed someone, and he was there? Can you think of a time when you were able to relieve the suffering of another, even though it took much time and effort on your part? Can you think of a time when you shared Christ with someone, which resulted in his becoming a Christian?

How can we learn to cultivate these open relationships in which we open our hearts and reveal our soul's deepest needs, give of ourselves—stripped of all pretenses, and lay masks aside?

1. *Don't be afraid to let others know when you need help.* Admit your weaknesses, your problems, and your challenges. Ask for prayer support.

I once visited a friend after the very difficult birth of her baby. A Caesarean had been performed, during which my friend's blood pressure had plunged so low that her life had been threatened. Upon awakening, she felt extremely ill and depressed. She has mentioned that during the days after her ordeal, she could almost physically feel the prayer support of her Christian friends, describing it as if hands were underneath her, physically lifting her up from a deep pit.

That feeling of support comes when we are open enough to ask for and receive the encouragement and strength that others give in times of need.

> Two are better than one, because they have a good return for their work: If one falls down, his friend can help him up. But pity the man who falls and has no one to help him up! Also, if two lie down together, they will keep warm. But how can one keep warm alone? (Ecclesiastes 4:9-11).

2. *Don't be afraid of your emotions.* Shedding tears and experiencing anger and frustration are not signs of weakness. You are a human, made in God's image; thus, you are capable of being hurt and of feeling emotional pain. To take that pain and persistently internalize it is damaging to your physical body and can cause all manner of psychological problems.

David was a strong, capable man. Yet, he expressed deep frustration and remorse in Psalm 31:9, 10: "Be merciful to me, O Lord, for I am in distress; my eyes grow weak with sorrow, my soul and my body with grief. My life is consumed by anguish, and my years by groaning; my strength fails because of my affliction, and my bones grow weak."

Those words are not the words of a man hiding behind a mask! David poured out his heart's deepest yearnings to his God and admit-

ted his distress and anguish. When we remove
a mask and reveal our suffering to another, we
open the channel through which healing love
may flow.

I'd just come from teaching a group of Christian ladies. During the course of the evening,
something was said or read that moved the
spirit of one who was suffering from the recent
death of a loved one. As her tears flowed, others
picked up her grief, and it became as their
own. I could almost visibly see a bond forming,
a protective shell enveloping the group. Masks
were shed. The spirit of God was moving.

3. *Be a shelter to those who are suffering.*

> This is how we know what love is:
> Jesus Christ laid down his life for us. And
> we ought to lay down our lives for our
> brothers. If anyone has material posses-
> sions and sees his brother in need but has
> no pity on him, how can the love of God
> be in Him. Dear children, let us not love
> with words or tongue but with actions
> and in truth (1 John 3:16-18).

My strong belief has always been that God
involves us for a purpose in the lives of those
who are suffering. He works His healing through
us. He uses us to comfort, to encourage, to
counsel, and to show love and concern.

Praise be to the God and Father of our Lord Jesus Christ, the Father of compassion and the God of all comfort, who comforts us in all our troubles, so that we can comfort those in any trouble with the comfort we ourselves have received from God. For just as the sufferings of Christ flow over into our lives, so also through Christ our comfort overflows (2 Corinthians 1:3,4).

Carry each other's burdens, and in this way you will fulfill the law of Christ (Galatians 6:2).

Each of you should look not only to your own interests, but also to the interests of others (Philippians 2:4).

Time, effort and commitment are required of you to share your life with others. When you are exhausted from caring for others, or when you feel the burden is growing too strong, you can turn to the Lord, who through His Holy Spirit will give you the strength you need, if you but ask.

About 10 years ago an older friend lost her husband to cancer. She had no children and few close relatives. I felt compelled to share in her pain and suffering and committed myself to that purpose.

Every day for several months, I rushed home after school, put my supper on, left my children in the care of my husband, and went to her home. I taught her to cross-stitch; I took her shopping; I sat for endless hours comforting her as she wept about the loss of her beloved husband. I often felt as though I were pulling her out of a deep well. At times she slipped back a little deeper, and I would pull a little harder.

During that period, I laid other things aside to help in her healing process. Many asked if I was fatigued. I was not; in fact, I felt renewed and refreshed. During that time God's mercies seemed new every morning. When He guides His children to help in the life of another, He provides the needed strength!

4. *Don't be afraid to admit your mistakes.*

"Therefore confess your sins to each other and pray for each other so that you may be healed" (James 5:16).

When we project an image of invincibility, people feel uncomfortable and intimidated by our presence. When we remove the mask and let them know that we also make mistakes, we are bonded together in our weakness. We are kindred spirits.

5. *Be available.* Cultivating open relationships means giving up "I'm-too-busy" excuses. Let people know you are willing to give your time.

On more than one occasion, I've been guilty of selfishness. I resent the intrusion of the telephone during an evening at home or of anything else that intrudes on my privacy. One evening I was forced to give up precious time to help a young lady contemplating suicide. She was a mere acquaintance in graduate school with me. She was 21 years old and disillusioned with life. Her husband was abusive, and she was suffering from acute depression. Her husband had just stormed out of her home, smashing a window in his anger.

When she called to talk to me, I resented the time I was going to have to sacrifice for her needs. So, I breathed a quick prayer for guidance, took a deep breath, and plunged in to help alleviate her suffering through love and encouragement.

She hung up three hours later, refusing to give me her address or telephone number, yet still threatening suicide. I can still hear the question she repeated over and over: "Does it hurt to die?"

I called the police, but they could do little without an address. Her parents lived in another city, and she was a stranger in town.

I slept little that night; most of it I spent in prayer. Early the next morning I inquired at the university, found her address, and spent the day with her. She finally agreed to give me her parents' telephone number, and that evening they arrived to take care of her. I never heard from her again, for she withdrew from school and simply vanished, leaving no forwarding address.

I was drained physically and emotionally from those tense hours, but they served a purpose. I feel sure that I helped save a life. Never again will I resent the intrusion of another into my life.

That's what open relationships are all about— being available, sacrificing when necessary, putting others' needs before your own, taking off the mask so you can remove the mask of another and then lend a helping hand.

My prayer since then has often been this:

> Dear heavenly Father, as I strip off the masks, I realize I am at the same time peeling off layers of selfishness and pride, exposing a sensitive vulnerability that could bring great pain.
>
> What's underneath the years of accumulated debris? Will I be able to recognize the "real" me?
>
> I'm going to feel bare and empty, but because I believe I am on the planet that You created in order to shed a small ray of light to the lost and suffering, I am willing to let go of the masks—maybe not all at once—but gently, guided by the Holy Spirit. Help me to replace the masks

with the crown of your lordship in my
life. In Jesus' name, Amen.

Lesson Nine

Questions

1. Name some occasions when you wore a mask for
   the sake of others.
2. Is it possible that we might practice unfair judgment when a Christian begins to shed his mask?
   Give a specific example.
3. What are the implications for the church when
   we practice open relationships?
4. In spite of admonitions and commands to help
   one another, does the time come when help must
   cease? Give specific examples.

In these first nine lessons, we've noted many of the things that are wrong with the world in which we live. We've been pretty hard on ourselves and on society. The rest of this book will be devoted to those values and beliefs that count for eternity, the things we should be pursuing with unending zeal and fervor. We can close out the negative chapters of our lives as we strive to live under the lordship of Jesus Christ and learn to triumph over life's trivia.

Lesson Ten

Knowing God— the Greatest Pursuit

I never cease to be amazed at the spiraling popularity of public figures who claim that the only thing important in life is the pursuit of self-knowledge. Just last week on a popular TV talk show, the hostess interviewed six women, all of whom had turned from a life concerned with others to a life centered on self, a philosophy we might call "me-ism." In a closing statement, one guest remarked, "There is *nothing* as important as making yourself happy. No one else matters—for you can find true happiness only in yourself."

As I mature in years and wisdom, I am more convinced than ever that the only important pursuit in life is not knowing myself, but knowing God: "Oh that we might know the Lord! Let us press on to know Him and He will respond to us as surely as the coming of dawn" (Hosea 6:3 KJV).

In Him I can find the only answer to the problems of a world shackled with sin—a world bowing under the pressure of a "give-me, give-me, give-me" society. As I read the papers and watch the news, I am tempted to weep as the prophet Jeremiah did when he found himself in the middle of a world that had turned from God—a people who through their greed and sinfulness found themselves spiraling towards self-destruction. In his frustration Jeremiah wrote, "O that my head were a spring of water and my eyes a fountain of tears! I would weep day and night for the slain of my people" (Jeremiah 9:1).

I experienced similar grief for my world as I watched a TV special about witchcraft. The show pointed out that thousands of our population are involved in the cult of Satanism.

I also viewed an update on the AIDS epidemic. The next morning a major university in Nashville reported that it has made available in dormitories machines which distribute free of charge "protection" for those who wish to participate in sexual activities.

Can we still say "God's in His heaven—all's right with the world?" This world in which we live is tumbling with great speed towards its own self-destruction. One minister describes the United States as being on a giant mud-slide to hell. The moral decadence of its people could be attributed to one thing: We are a people who do not *know* God. God gave Jeremiah the same reason in Jeremiah 9:3: " '. . . and they do not know me,' declared the Lord."

I know my family, my friends, the children I teach, my neighbors, my community, world personalities, good literature, and the latest movies, but do I really know God? Do I really understand Him and His purpose for my life? Do I see my life through the lens of His vision? Do I accept whatever happens to me as given by God and under His surveillance? Do I really *want* to know Him with a deep, all-consuming desire that fills every thread of my being?

A lady once gave a negative review of a book she had read. Later, she met the author, fell in love with him, and married him. Naturally, her opinion of the book changed, and she reported that his book was the best she had ever read.

When we personally *know* the Author of the most important Book in the world, that book miraculously changes from one of history and facts to an alive, vibrant account of a loving God who takes care of His people.

In the book of Hebrews, God tells about the covenant He will make with the house of Israel:

> I will put my laws in their minds, and write them on their hearts. I will be their God, and they will be my people. No longer will a man teach his neighbor, or a man his brother, saying, "Know the

Lord," because they will all know me,
from the least to them to the greatest
(Hebrews 8:10-12).

How much difference it would make in our
world if "all" really knew God, from the least
to the greatest!

I once asked the children in my classroom
to draw a picture of how they saw God. One
child drew an elaborate picture of an old gentleman with a long, flowing beard, seated on a
throne. Around him were many switches, each
one labeled with names such as "thunder,"
"lightning," and "rain." God's long arms were
stretched out, and He was saying, "Which switch
shall I pull today?"

What is your visual image of God? I asked
this to the ladies in a Bible class. Some of their
responses were very interesting.

> I see God in a long, white, flowing robe,
> but He's not a feeble old man. He's got
> brown hair and a beard and looks 35-40.
> He is a huge figure that stands just above
> the sky. At other times I picture Him
> sitting on a huge throne in a colossal
> throne room, and I am walking up to the
> throne to talk to Him. In both instances,
> He is loving and understanding, but I
> always know that His word is the last
> word. He seems very real when I'm out
> in a beautiful place in nature . . . .

I picture God as a very big man inhabiting a place with lots of clouds. He has a very long white beard with piercing eyes, and there are angels everywhere with harps. He sits in a seat that looks like a judge's seat in a courtroom. He has a very big book on His desk with a big feather pen.

I see a vague figure of God with His raiment of white flowing with the breeze. As I talk, the angels listen compassionately. When I've asked for forgiveness, shouts of glory rise from heaven . . . .

God is everywhere I look—in trees, mountains, streams, and the sky. He is a bright light that always smiles. . . .

A common thread runs through most people's concept of God. The words "warm," "gentle" and "compassionate" are often used to describe God.

Is your image of God the same as it was 10 years ago? You wouldn't likely be studying this book if you did not already have a loving relationship with the Father. But what *kind* of relationship is it? What does it really mean to *know* God?

Let's begin by correcting some popular misconceptions.

1. *Knowing God is not just knowing who He is.* Most of us have studied *about* God since

childhood. We know lots of facts, and we have created a visual image and an intellectual definition of this God we worship. We use such words as "creator of the world, omnipotent, omniscient, omnipresent, eternal and everlasting" to describe Him. But knowing facts *about* God doesn't mean we know *Him.*

Below are the last words written by King David before his death. They paint a beautiful picture of God!

> Praise be to you, O Lord, God of our father Israel, from everlasting to everlasting. Yours, O Lord, is the greatness and the power and the glory and the majesty and the splendor, for everything in heaven and earth is yours. Yours, O Lord, is the kingdom; you are exalted as head over all. Wealth and honor come from you; you are the ruler of all things. In your hands are strength and power to exalt and give strength to all. Now, our God, we give you thanks, and praise your glorious name (1 Chronicles 29:10-13).

2. *Knowing God is not just keeping all the rules.* The rich young ruler, when he asked Jesus how to have eternal life, told Him he had kept all the commandments from his youth up. The Jewish code of behavior contained more than 600 laws and regulations. The Pharisees were diligent to keep all the rules but were caught

up in legalism. They were hypocrites, pretending to be God's people, yet Jesus said they didn't know God.

We assemble with the church three times a week, take the Lord's Supper every Sunday, pray every day, and so on, but is this *knowing* God?

3. *Knowing God is not just being baptized into His family.* Christians can be in God's family almost an entire lifetime, yet still not *know* God.

I was baptized at the tender age of 12. As a preteen, I had been exposed to many enriching spiritual experiences through Christian camp and an active, vibrant church that was eager to help its young people get to know God. I already had a meaningful relationship with my Father— as deep as my immature years would allow. That relationship was a simplistic, child-like one of trust, and it carries many of the same characteristics 40 years later. But my baptism was only the beginning of a journey that has taken me over mountains and through valleys time and time again. Through each year my faith has deepened and my love for God has grown.

When an adopted child goes home with his or her parents for the first time, he doesn't *know* them on a deep, personal level. A loving parental bond develops over years. As "adopted" children of our heavenly Father, we require years to build a deep personal relationship with Him.

God has always been concerned with a personal relationship with His people. He desired a loving relationship with Adam and Eve in the garden, but sin separated them. In the New Testament, God made possible a new covenant of relationships through redemption, desiring always to dwell with His people.

As you read these words, you may believe that something is missing in your relationship with the Father. Perhaps you are not quite sure what this walk is. You want to know this great God in a deep exciting way. Let's get "back to the basics" in the next lessons, so we can know God.

Lesson Ten

Questions

1. Look up the following verses, and fill in the blanks with a word or phrase from each passage that describes God:
   Isaiah 5:16 _____
   Isaiah 6:3 _____
   Romans 6:23 _____
   1 Corinthians 13 _____
   John 3:16 _____

2. Share with one another your visual and intellectual images of God.
3. Think about your baptism. How has your relationship with God changed since that event? Do you feel closer to God now?
4. What are some of the "rules" we believe must be kept in order to gain favor with God?
5. Why is "keeping rules" not enough?
6. Discuss the concept of "me-ism." Relate incidents in TV programming, politics, religion, and other areas, where this ego-centered philosophy is evident.

Lesson Eleven

Back to the Basics

Dedication and hard work were required for the Pharisees to be able to keep the hundreds of laws bound on them by the Jewish religion. Jesus, with His divine wisdom, took all those laws and compacted them into the two simple commandments found in Matthew 22:37-40:

> One of them, an expert in the law, tested him with this question: "Teacher, which is the greatest commandment in the Law?" Jesus replied: " 'Love the Lord your God with all your heart and with all your soul and with all your mind.' This is the first and greatest commandment. And the second is like it: 'Love your neighbor as yourself.' All the Law and the Prophets hang on these two commandments."

The Pharisees probably mumbled among themselves, "Come on; that's too simple!" Those commands sound simple to us, too; yet, when we take them apart and look at them step by step, the "simplicity" takes on new meanings and added responsibilities.

1. *Knowing God means that you love Him with all your heart, soul and mind* (Matthew 22:37). We must love God with our emotions, our spirits and our intellects. We take pleasure in Him: "Delight in the Almighty, and lift up your face to God" (Job 22:26).

To say that we love God with our heart, soul and mind is to make a "pledge of allegiance" to God, to yield to His divine and sovereign will. Paul and the Old Testament prophets said that "God is the potter and we are the clay" (Romans 9:21). Yielding means depending, in the childlike trust, knowing that God will work out the circumstances so that good will come, now or later (Romans 8:28). Yielding means giving ourselves into the care of God just as a newborn gives itself to the care of its parents, knowing instinctively that it will be taken care of.

To love God means to place His will above family, friends and other commitments. We will turn from self and from seeking what we want to God, to worship Him in the fullness of our spirits: "If . . . you turn your foot from doing your own pleasure . . . desisting from your own ways, from seeking your own pleasure, and speaking your own word, then you will take delight in the Lord" (Isaiah 58:13, 14 NASB).

When we love God with all our hearts, we lay aside the trivial pursuits of this world and count everything as loss but knowing God.

Loving God means we will have a personal relationship with Him. The apostles had eaten, slept, traveled and lived with Jesus 24 hours a day for three years, and yet Jesus knew their relationship with Him was incomplete: "If you really knew me, you would know my Father as well" (John 14:7).

If we really *know* God, He will be our constant companion, our friend, our counselor, our refuge, and our strength. We will think of Him during the day, pray to Him, and lean on Him for every decision.

The pursuit of this love takes dedication, self-discipline and commitment. Time must be spent in fellowship with Him through His Word and prayer. Pursuing deep love for God means reorganizing our priorities. The result of such a love is a religion that is bright and meaningful, a religion in which the heart is filled with joy and excitement and we sing, pray and work out of love, not duty or habit. This love is worth pursuing!

2. *Loving God means we have a genuine love for our neighbors.* Christ, the psychologist, knew that at the root of all sin is love of self—the

"me-ism" mentioned earlier. Real effort and commitment are required if we are to take the same quantity of love we have for self and shower it on others. Some thoughts from *Leaves of God* provided insight into the relationship between love for God and love for neighbors.

> Love your neighbor for God's sake, and God for your own sake, who created all things for your sake, and redeemed you for His mercy's sake. If your love hath any other motive, it is false love; if your motive hath any other end, it is self-love. If you neglect your love to your neighbor, in vain you profess your love of God; for by your love of God, your love to your neighbor is acquired; and by your love to your neighbor, your love of God is nourished.[1]

As Christians made in the image of a holy God, we are to be a mirror of His love and mercy to all mankind. Because we live in His presence at all times and because He has blessed us abundantly, we must expand our thinking beyond self and family to include others who need care but are unable to have it. These people are the neighbors about whom Christ is talking in verse 38. To love them as much as we love ourselves is the key expression of a Christian heart.

To love my neighbor means I yield myself to the needs and interests of others, just as God gave Himself for my needs as a sinner. "When we were still powerless, Christ died for the ungodly . . . But God demonstrates his own love for us in this: While we were still sinners, Christ died for us" (Romans 5:6).

To love others means I will be sensitive to their needs and ready to let the love of God flow through me to them.

This commandment is tough. You might be thinking, "Let me start somewhere else, Lord, maybe I can give more, or teach a class, or join the church visitation team, but to love my neighbor as myself, I can't do it!"

The commandment is tough because people are tough. Frederick the Great said, "The more I get to know people, the more I love my dog!"

You might be surprised to know that love is not always a feeling. We are not required to *feel* good about all our neighbors. But we are committed to exhibiting the love of God through compassion for our neighbors.

> Therefore, as God's chosen people, holy and dearly loved, clothe yourselves with compassion, kindness, humility, gentleness and patience (Colossians 3:12).

So, who are my neighbors? My neighbors include the homeless, the poor, the elderly, those who might be handicapped, single parents, widows, and low-income families with children to feed and clothe.

The Scriptures have much to say about the poor and God's concern for them. He commanded special care for them in the Old Testament. Through Isaiah, God said this:

> Is not this the kind of fasting I have chosen: to loose the chains of injustice and untie the cords of the yoke, to set the oppressed free and break every yoke? Is it not to share your food with the hungry and to provide the poor wanderer with shelter—when you see the naked, to clothe him, and not to turn away from your own flesh and blood? (Isaiah 58:7, 8).

God goes on to give a beautiful promise to those who show concern for the poor:

> And if you spend yourselves in behalf of the hungry and satisfy the needs of the oppressed, then your light will rise in the darkness, and your night will become like the noonday. The Lord will guide you always; he will satisfy your needs in a sun-scorched land and will strengthen your frame. You will be like a well-watered garden, like a spring whose waters never fail (Isaiah 58:10, 11).

Jesus loved and ministered to the poor. He looked at the multitudes of people and felt compassion (Matthew 9:36). We have the same responsibility as we seek the kingdom of God.

Be aware that Satan is not going to make it easy for you to love your neighbor. He will delight in putting competition in your way and he will compete by using our busyness, our conceit and our self-centeredness.

Busyness. The "curse" of our culture is busyness. It gets in the way of almost every service we wish to perform for our Lord. We're busy making money, acquiring things, dreaming, and hurrying to and fro. All these activities count for nothing.

Because we're so busy, we cling to the time-worn excuse "I'll do it tomorrow." Somehow this excuse eases the guilt of knowing a certain task should be done today. We seem to think the tomorrows will keep on and on until we have *just enough* time left to do everything we had planned.

And then, when all the tomorrows have been used, the agonizing cry of "too late" will take its place. Several years ago, I recorded my thoughts about time's passing.

Too late . . .
  to say "I'm sorry"
  to hug a child
  to cheer a lonely widow
Too late . . .
  to talk to a neighbor about Christ
  to "hunger and thirst" for His Word
  to accept Him as Lord
Too late . . .
  to say "Thank you"
  to take back ugly words spoken in haste
  to help a friend in need
Too late . . .
  to talk to God.
No more tomorrows . . .
No more excuses . . .
  Only the silent, dark emptiness
  And the heartbreaking sound of millions of souls breathing in unison the agonizing words . . .
            TOO LATE!

Conceit. Have you ever thought you were "too good" to give of yourself to others? Perhaps you elevate your nose a little when you walk by the homeless scattered in the streets of a large city. I've done that very thing. I've become hardened to the poor in our midst, thinking that their poverty is a result of laziness or lack of education. Like many, I've become oblivious to them, locking myself in my own comfortable world.

Or, perhaps, there's someone with whom you just can't get along. Perhaps your spirit has been buffeted by angry words or deeds. You refuse to forgive.

Refusing to forgive is simply refusing to love God.

Self-Centeredness. The opposite of biblical love, in which I give myself away, is self-centeredness. When I'm self-centered, I heap life upon myself. I want everything, and I want everyone to love me. The phenomenal "me disease" is sweeping across our country. Are you one of its victims?

Try waking up this week with the following words on your lips and heart: "I wonder who I can bless today?"

The Blessings of Knowing God

We've learned what God requires of us. And He promises this: "Seek first his kingdom and his righteousness, and all these things will be given to you as well" (Matthew 6:33). Many blessings come from knowing this great God:

1. *We will become like Him.* Because He is holy, I want to be holy. Because He is good, I want to be good. Because He is love, I want to be more loving.

After many years of married life, some couples begin to look alike. Children take on the physical and emotional characteristics of their parents. When we really *know* God, the more we will become like Him: "Be holy, because I am holy" (1 Peter 1:16).

2. *Knowing God makes us strong.* When we live each day under the all-wise, powerful hand of the Creator, we can take each step in bold confidence, knowing His love covers us, surrounds us, enfolds us, and gives us the strength to face any circumstance: "My times are in your hands . . . " (Psalm 31:15). "God is our refuge and strength, an ever-present help in trouble" (Psalm 46:1).

When we know God, we can come before His throne and lay everything down in total submission—every burden, every care, and every hurt—and we know He will take each situation and work it out for good. We can wait patiently for the outcome: "But they that wait upon the Lord shall renew their strength; they shall mount up with wings like eagles; they shall run, and not be weary; and they shall walk, and not faint" (Isaiah 40:31 *KJV*).

David had so much confidence when he prayed this:

In Thee, O Lord, I have taken refuge;
let me never be ashamed; in Thy righ-

teousness deliver me. Incline Thine ear
to me, rescue me quickly, be Thou to me
a rock of strength, a stronghold to save
me. For Thou art my rock and my fortress;
for Thy name's sake Thou wilt lead me
and guide me. Thou wilt pull me out of
the net which they have secretly laid for
me; for Thou art my strength (Psalm 31:
1-4 *KJV*).

3. *Knowing God helps us understand eternal
life.* "This is eternal life: that they may know
you, the only true God, and Jesus Christ, whom
you have sent" (John 17:3).

If we know that God is and that He will
reward those who diligently seek Him, then we
can believe that a better place is waiting for us
at the end of this life: "And it is appointed
unto man once to die, but after this the judge-
ment" (Hebrews 9:27 *NKJB*).

When we finally come to it, death will be
just another expression of God's unbounded
love and beauty. It will be a place of perfect
peace where we can enjoy the presence of the
Lord forever and ever and where will be no
more tears, death, sadness, crying, disease or
temptation: "Things which eye has not seen and
ear has not heard; and which have not entered
the heart of man, all that God has prepared for
those who love Him" (1 Corinthians 2:9).

Perhaps we should add "to those who *know* Him."

Lesson Eleven

Questions

1. What are some things we do out of duty rather than love?
2. How can we love God with heart, soul and mind?
3. Can helping others ever become a sin?
4. How does serving others nourish a love of God?
5. When (under what circumstances) do you have the most problem loving your neighbor?
6. What are some specific ways your class can help those in need—single mothers, widows, the homeless, and others you name?

Notes Lesson Eleven

[1]*Leaves of Gold* (Williamsport, PA: Coslett Publishing Co.) 1960, p. 117.

Lesson Twelve

To Hear the Song Again

Have you ever wanted to shout, "Stop the world; I want to get off"? Indeed, we're living in a crazy world—a world in which we pursue wealth, possessions, a beautiful body and success. On top of it all, we want to be "supermoms." We want to hold down full-time jobs outside the home and still supply the physical and emotional needs of our entire families who are immaculately dressed, have spotless homes, and serve various community organizations and committees at school, among other things!

To some degree we *are* all superwomen or supermoms. But we have two traits in common: We're all exhausted, and we're tired of running, running, running!

Ask yourself these questions:

- When was the last time you celebrated life? (I celebrate a good night's rest.)
- When was the last time you awakened eager and fresh to start a new day? (I play a

game with my trusty alarm clock every morning. I give it a friendly tap, and it gives me 15 additional minutes of sleep!)

- When was the last time you laughed so hard you couldn't stop?
- Do the simple pleasures of life seem to be eluding you?

It appears as though one morning we awaken, and the world has lost some of its beauty. We seem to have lost the joyous strains of the symphony of life. At such times, we must lay aside the trivial concerns of this earthly kingdom and seek the kingdom of God.

Tony Campolo, in *Who Switched the Price Tags?*, compares our mixed-up value system to a situation in which one goes into a department store, finds two items—one of great value and one very inexpensive—and switches the price tags.[1] Daily we make sacrifices for things of little lasting value, ignoring at the same time those things which are deserving, such as friendship, family, home, and fellowship with God. The trade-off is unrewarding, for without these, the joyful strains of life's song fades into a barely audible hum.

Jesus wants us to lead a rich, rewarding life of abundance: "I have come that you might have life, and have it more abundantly" (John 10:10).

The abundant life He's speaking of is the "good" life we've been pursuing. But, like hikers lost in a vast wilderness, we're following all the wrong paths. A good life does not consist of wealth, possessions, a beautiful body, a luxurious home or worldly success.

1. *The abundant life is a life of acceptance.* Daily we're faced with pressures unknown to any previous society. Bad times are getting worse, and relief doesn't seem to be in sight. Habbakuk must have felt that as he waited for Judah's oppressors to destroy Jerusalem:

> Although the fig tree shall not blossom, neither shall fruit be in the vines; the labour of the olive shall fail, and the fields shall yield no meat; the flock shall be cut off from the fold, and there shall be no herd in the stalls (Habbakuk 3:17 *KJV*).

He goes on, though, to remember that God in every circumstance gives reason for rejoicing:

> Yet I will rejoice in the Lord, I will joy in the God of my salvation. The Lord God is my strength, and he will make my feet like hinds' feet, and he will make me to walk upon mine high places . . . (Habakkuk 3:17-19 *KJV*).

After all, God didn't promise we'd be leading

at halftime; He promised we'd be winning at the end! Paul said it this way:

> I have fought the good fight, I have finished the race, I have kept the faith. Finally, there is laid up for me the crown of righteousness, which the Lord, the righteous Judge, will give me on that day; and not to me only, but also to all who have loved His appearing (2 Timothy 4:7, 8 *NKJV*).

Sometimes we find it difficult to accept what life has to offer, but the abundant life in Jesus Christ demands that we avoid the temptation of always wishing for more—a better home, nicer clothes or new furniture. In accepting the good life, we learn to accept life with all its imperfect flaws and shortcomings and to give God the glory!

2. *The abundant life is rich in family and home.* Husband and children come first, before community projects and, yes, even before church projects. We are to do nothing to take away from our relationship with our children. We are to be actively involved in things they enjoy doing. Each year I have students' parents whom I never meet, even on the telephone. They don't return notes I send home to have signed, and they never look at their child's work. They don't sign up for parent-teacher conferences, and they don't

even come to special programs put on by their children.

Children are a heritage of the Lord, and if we don't meet their emotional needs in the first years of life, later they won't want us around to share in *any* of their life experiences!

3. *The abundant life is a simple life.* Before we can have a simple life, we have to clean out the clutter. Almost daily we have to clear the odds and ends that accumulate in our homes through carelessness and neglect. In search of the abundant life, we have to sweep away the clutter of frivolous, energy-demanding tasks and responsibilities to find a simple lifestyle—a way of living in which God is glorified through daily worship, constant communication through prayer and study, simple service, and trust.

To live a simple life requires that we remove the blinders and open our eyes to truly see the glories of God's creation. They have been given to us free of charge by the great gift-giver, and they can bring more joy and happiness than any amount of wealth or worldly possessions.

Last summer my family and I spent several days in the Blue Ridge Mountains. Our lodging was a small, simple inn perched on the side of a mountain. When we arrived, rain was falling, and the mountains were shrouded in a blanket of fog. Later that afternoon the rain stopped, and the fog began to rise, opening the curtain on a panorama of soft mountain ridges visible for miles. We were silent, breathing in the riches that lay before us.

Words are inadequate at such times, so we watched the great unveiling in silence. As the sun began to shine in splendor upon the rolling hills and mountains of the Blue Ridge, I felt like a member of the royal family feasting at a sumptuous banquet.

I stayed a long time on the balcony, soaking in the peaceful scene. Burdens and tension began to fall off as though I were shedding layers of cumbersome clothing. I could easily share in the feelings of the psalmist as he wrote, "Who is like the Lord our God, the One who sits enthroned on high, who stoops down to look on the heaven and the earth" (Psalm 113:5, 6)? And he wrote, "From the heaven the Lord looks down and sees all mankind; from his dwelling place He watches all who live on earth—he ... considers everything they do" (Psalm 33: 13-15).

I could imagine my God, sitting daily with chin in hand, pondering each of my activities and all of my thoughts, fears, dreams and hopes. How He must be growing weary of my hectic lifestyle—my senseless running to and fro "chasing the wind"!

This God of the mountain was a simple God, and the mountains spoke of a simple lifestyle, rich in beauty and majesty. I knew my task was to bring this God into the city, my classroom, and my home.

I began to view my life through His eyes, analyzing it as to ways in which I could unclutter it. I came up with the following suggestions, which, by the way, I have incorporated into my life successfully:

a. Learn to let go of some of the demands you place on yourself, such as a spotless and decorated home and meals that take all day to prepare.

b. Learn to say "no" to anything that gets in the way of time with your God and your family.

c. Simplify the lives of your children. Children do not *have* to take every private lesson that is offered in your community! Do they have to play on the soccer team *every* year? We desire that our children be well-rounded and able to excel in many areas, but of much more benefit to them is a calm, happy household in which Mom walks—not runs—through her day with grace and serenity. She can't do that if she is running a taxi service to various after-school lessons and activities!

d. Block in time on your calendar when you can have time *by yourself*—alone with God in a quiet, serene setting.

e. Commit your daily calendar to Him. Ask for His wisdom to weed out and

destroy those things that are keeping you
from functioning at your very best.

4. *The abundant life is a brief life, walked
in wisdom.* I had to reset my digital alarm clock.
I watched as the hours quickly rolled from a.m.
to p.m. "That's how fast my life seems to be
passing," I thought. David noticed it, too, when
he wrote this: "As for man, his days are as
grass; as a flower of the field, so he flourisheth.
For the wind passeth over it and it is gone, and
the place thereof shall know it no more" (Psalm
103:15, 16).

Death itself can show us the way to abundant
life. When we lose a loved one, we're brought
face to face with the uncertainty of time on
earth. Moments with loved ones and friends
become dear. Eyes are opened to previously
unseen beauty.

When we learn how to die, we will learn how
to live, for death's lessons have much to teach
us: "Better is the day of death than the day of
one's birth. It is better to go to the house of
mourning, than to go to the house of feasting;
for that is the end of all men; and the living
will lay it to his heart. Sorrow is better than
laughter; for by the sadness of the countenance
the heart is made better" (Ecclesiastes 7:1-4
KJV).

Our time on earth is brief and to be cherished. Each new day brings new growth, new insight and new awareness—a stone in the path of growth. Such is the "abundant" life in Christ.

5. *The abundant life is a joyous life and must involve some risk.* God wants us to be joyful always. When we awaken each morning, we should create the mood of the day, rather than let circumstances create our mood. Arising happy is a difficult task when someone you love is ill, or when your job is distasteful, or when no money is left to buy the next meal after paying the bills. Being joyful is difficult when your husband has left you with three small children to raise, or when you discover your child is a homosexual.

At those times we have to squeeze a tiny drop of joy out of the simple things in life, such as the love of a friend, a call from someone who cares, or a brief note written to encourage and uplift. We have to learn to say, as the psalmist did, "I will say of the Lord, He is my refuge and my fortress, my God in whom I trust" (Psalm 91:2).

For me, few things can lift the gloom of a dreary day as can humor. The abundant life is one rich in humor, which is defined by one as "the unshakeable ability to break life up into little pieces and make it liveable." To be able to laugh at self and at impossible situations is an art, a discipline, a gift.

I teach third grade along with five other teachers. When we sit down to a quick lunch, we usually begin a contest to see whose nerves are the most frazzled. We relate all the disastrous events of the day and almost talk ourselves into a nervous frenzy. On every occasion, we will be rescued by Eve, who has the unusual talent of turning a disastrous event, such as a child throwing up on your desk, into hysterical mirth. We end up laughing at ourselves; our food digests better; and when time is up, we're ready to move on to better things.

Along with humor, the joyous life must involve certain risks. I once read that some people walk through life with gloves and a raincoat on, forever worrying about tomorrow or about the consequences of an action or deed of today. I must confess that I have the tendency to be one of those dreary people who goes about with all kinds of reasons for not taking risks and having fun. God would have us let go of senseless fears, take some risks, and worry about the pain later.

I did just that last spring in the mountains of Colorado, when I decided to fulfill a long-time dream of having a snowmobile ride. My hearty companions on this guided tour through the Arapaho National Forest were two of my husband's college debaters, who had come with us to Colorado for a national debate conference. They chose to go snowmobiling rather than take a simple skiing jaunt with my husband and daughter.

When I climbed on the snowmobile, my heart lurched. My hands trembled so much I couldn't turn on the throttle to engage the engine. I was ready to climb off (with some relief) when I was rescued by one of my young companions. He gave me a look of pity mingled with mischievous glee as, with one flick of the wrist, he started the motor. As it was too late to turn back, I was determined to take a risk and *live* this abundant life to the fullest.

During that drive to the top of a 6,000-foot mountain on a trail carved through 10-foot drifts of snow and around endless hairpin curves (at an outrageous speed of 35 to 40 mph), I was overcome with exhilaration at least every five minutes. At such times I had to sing loud, joyful praises to God. The fact that I was frightened silly and so cold that my entire body felt as if it were submerged in a frozen pond is insignificant.

The silent stillness of the snowy forest and the closeness I felt to God when my group stopped to witness the magnificent mountaintop view will linger in my memory for years.

I'm sure God was standing tall and proud as He watched this fearful child toss aside inhibitions and experience abundant life to the fullest!

The activities classified as "play" are not just for children. Play is part of the call to a simplistic style of living that brings the true meaning of life into focus.

If you want to hear the song of joyful living once more, take off your mask, become more involved in trying to improve your world, open your eyes to the beauty that surrounds you, simplify your life, fill your life with people who bring you joy and laughter, and don't be afraid to take a risk! Life is now, and it's temporary, so celebrate it while you can!

No one has expressed it more beautifully than W. Waldemar Argow, when he wrote "Wealth":

> To have a sense of appreciation that some things are of more value than others, and that inward assurance that the soul is good friends with what makes the birds sing, the flowers grow and the stars twinkle, lends a quiet, inward calm beside which other forms of pleasures and rewards are as nothingness itself.

> To earn a little, to spend a little less than one earns; to love and nurture a few living things . . . a shy little plant in the window, or an affectionate dog; to thrill at the sight of a morning sunbeam lacing itself through

the dinginess of your room; to own and often read a few dear old books until they grow as intimate as a prayer; to have a few understanding friends to whom you never need explain, and then to know how to keep that friendship in repair; to be able to entertain yourself with the memory of deeds done for themselves alone without any desire for reward or applause, and with thoughts that cluster like a wistaria round a noble purpose, and thus make fragrant your solitude; to be content with the homey things that are nearest—daily bread, daily loves, daily duties—so that you do not have to grasp at the stars for adventure; then at eventide a simple prayer with the benediction of sound sleep, while the silent stars keep vigil overhead, and the childlike trust that God is behind all . . . Ah, that is to live with plenty, which is just enough to make life what it should be . . . an adventure in happiness where one finds those precious things that neither age nor misfortune can snatch away![2]

Lesson Twelve

Questions

1. What are some excuses we give for not being happy? Do we delay happiness until some future time when everything will be going well?
2. Name some things in life in which we have "switched the price tag."
3. Jesus invited the rich young ruler to take up his cross and follow Him. What could the word "cross" mean in that statement?
4. Could we simplify public worship, or is it too simple?
5. In what areas of life could we simplify?
6. Share a time in which you have let go of fears and inhibitions and truly enjoyed life.
7. Is "play" only for children? Explain.

Other passages for meditation: Psalms 49; 103; 33:3; 73; 20; 40:1-10; and 46.

Notes Lesson 12

¹Tony Campolo, *Who Switched the Price Tags?* (Waco: Word Books), 1986, p. 13, 14.
²Source unknown.

A Final Word

One of my favorite hymns is "Crown Him with Many Crowns." In a stirring way it brings to remembrance a relationship with Jesus Christ in which He is crowned Lord above all, the one and only King, to be adored and magnified forever and ever.

Always dwelling on self and seeking a better life, we have taken the crowns that belong to Him and have placed them upon ourselves—the crown of self, of ego and pride, of glory and honor. We've sought riches and worldly success. Little has mattered but our climb up the road to bigger and better things.

We've forgotten the words of God spoken through Jeremiah:

> Let not the wise man boast of His wisdom; or the strong man boast of his strength; or the rich man boast of his riches, but let him who boasts boast about this: that he understands and knows me, that I am the Lord, who exercises kind-

ness, justice and righteousness on earth,
for in these I delight, declares the Lord
(Jeremiah 9:23, 24).

I pray that through the study of this book you
have been able to see through the trivial pursuits
of this life to a higher and loftier plain, in which
your daily pursuit is to know God and to love
Him. I pray you have been able to participate
in the noble pursuit of making this world a
better place in which to live.

Our concerns and efforts *can* make a difference. This aged, creaking world needs a host
of prayer warriors. Through Him we can overcome the evil forces that threaten to destroy the
ideals of honor and decency today and for
generations to come.

May the following verses spoken by the apos-
tle Paul be our prayer for one another as we
join together.

> For this reason I kneel before the Fa-
> ther, from whom his whole family in
> heaven and on earth derives its name. I
> pray that out of his glorious riches he
> may strengthen you with power through
> his spirit in your inner being, so that
> Christ might dwell in your hearts through
> faith. And I pray that you, being rooted
> and established in love, may have power,
> together with all the saints, to grasp how
> wide and long and high and deep is the
> love of Christ, and to know this love that

surpasses knowledge—that you may be filled to the measure of all the fullness of God (Ephesians 3:14-21).

May He be hailed as the matchless King who is leading us to the final triumph!

www.ingramcontent.com/pod-product-compliance
Lightning Source LLC
LaVergne TN
LVHW011205080426
835508LV00007B/609